YOOPERNATURAL HAUNTS

UPPER PENINSULA PARANORMAL RESEARCH SOCIETY CASE FILES

YOOPERNATURAL HAUNTS

UPPER PENINSULA PARANORMAL RESEARCH SOCIETY CASE FILES

By Brad Blair, Tim Ellis
and Steve LaPlaunt

Visionary Living Publishing/Visionary Living, Inc.
New Milford, Connecticut

Yoopernatural Haunts:
Upper Peninsula Paranormal Research Society Case Files

By Brad Blair, Tim Ellis and Steve LaPlaunt

Copyright 2019 by Brad Blair and Tim Ellis

Front cover design by April Slaughter
Back cover and interior design by Leslie McAllister

ISBN: 978-1-942157-51-9 (pbk)
ISBN: 978-1-942157-52-6 (epub)

Published by Visionary Living Publishing/Visionary Living, Inc.
New Milford, Connecticut
www.visionarylivingpublishing.com

TABLE OF CONTENTS

FOREWORD

Michigan's Upper Peninsula reigns as one of the most mysterious regions in the United States, and perhaps even in North America. Cradled by the mighty Great Lakes of Superior, Michigan, and Huron, and a stone's throw from Canada, this northern extremity of the state has a long and rich history. Harsh winters made it nearly inaccessible in the past, and only the hardiest of souls ventured into its deep forests and wind-lashed lake shores to settle and survive.

The Upper Peninsula has evolved almost in a world of its own. Even today, with tourists and seasonal visitors easily making their way in, the region has retained its unique personality. When you cross the breath-taking suspension bridge at the narrows of Michigan and Huron lakes, you know you have arrived "somewhere else."

That mystery applies to the ghosts, hauntings, and eerie legends as well as the land of the living. The Upper Peninsula is steeped in supernatural lore and phenomena, full of energy that pulses just below the threshold of ordinary reality.

There are no better paranormal investigators to plumb these spooky depths than the Upper Peninsula Paranormal Research Society, most of whose members are natives who are rooted in the land and understand its vibrations.

I became friends with the UPPRS team some years ago when they invited me to participate in their annual MIParacon in Sault Ste. Marie. At first glance, one might think that the northern tip of Michigan would be an unlikely place to stage a paranormal event, but it is an ideal place for the reasons aforementioned. The MIParacon has grown into a juggernaut every August, and I have been pleased to be a regular part of it. I've explored some of the terrain as well and can attest to the magic the Upper Peninsula holds.

In this their debut book, the UPPRS team presents some of their most interesting paranormal cases. They make the places and personalities come alive. Reading the histories and stories is like being transported back in time. What I especially appreciate are the accounts of how the team approaches an investigation. They are methodical and professional, and it's fascinating as a reader to look over their shoulders as they experience and document phenomena. They also have a good time. You'll learn a lot about paranormal investigation here—real investigation, not the exaggerated antics of "reality television."

You can visit all the places in this book and soak up the haunted atmospheres. Take in a meal or two. You might catch a glimpse of a phantom from the long-ago past or hear ghostly sounds of voices and activities belonging to bygone days. You might just run into one of the UPPRS team as well!

—Rosemary Ellen Guiley author, *The Encyclopedia of Ghosts and Spirits* and 70 other books on the paranormal

Introduction
How It All Started

Many people ask how or why does a person become a "ghost hunter" or "paranormal researcher." The answer to that question can be as varied and individualized as the many personalities in the field today. For some, it's a search for answers to questions that remain unattained and mysteries to us all. For others it was a paranormal experience at an early age. Some are drawn to the thrill and adrenaline rush of fear, which once experienced first-hand is hard to replicate.

In recent years, with cable television introducing a plethora of paranormal reality shows, there seems to be a thought process that this is a field that will make you rich and famous. For the Upper Peninsula Paranormal Research Society (UPPRS), that question can be summed up with one simple but powerful word: Friends. We would like to share some of our most memorable encounters and locations with you but first, you should know how it all began.

Growing up in Michigan's Upper Peninsula can be an adventure all its own. For those unfamiliar with the area, the Upper Peninsula (or simply U.P.) consists of the top one-third of Michigan's land mass; however only three percent of the state's population call this area home. It is surrounded by lakes Michigan and Huron to the south and Lake Superior to the north. The U.P. is a land of thick forests, undeveloped waterfront, and four distinct seasons; a place where people can easily lose themselves in nature; a true outdoorsman's dream.

Being a unique and somewhat isolated territory, the U.P. came to develop its own legends and folklore; often a mixture of tales handed down from French voyageurs, Finnish settlers, and the legends of the Native American tribes who have inhabited the peninsula for many centuries. Children spend summer nights around campfires being told tales of wild men roaming the forest, lake monsters terrorizing sailors, and ghosts haunting abandoned lumber camps, all intended to provide a good fright. Other, less chilling stories are also passed along of benevolent supernatural beings: Bearwalkers (native shapeshifters) who could use their powers to the benefit of their tribe, nature spirits who have been said to lead lost explorers to safety, and Bloodstoppers, people who can stop a wound from bleeding by simply laying on hands or reciting a chant, are just a few examples of these beneficial presences said to inhabit the U.P.

Brad Blair, Steve LaPlaunt, and Tim Ellis founded the UPPRS. Each of them was born and raised in Sault Ste. Marie, Michigan, located at the far eastern side of the U.P., and they have been childhood friends since elementary school. The lore of local legends, ghosts, ghouls, and anything else that went bump in the night fascinated them at an early age. They spent hours at the local library reading titles such as *Scary Stories to Tell in the Dark* and combing through the kids' horror section, as well as listening to Pickwick vinyl records of Halloween sound effects and stories year-round. They were the kids telling ghost stories at sleepovers and on the back of the school bus. Watching *Creature Feature* on Saturday afternoons on television was a weekly event. This shared interest bonded the trio at an early age. Many children were and are fascinated with the same stories, cartoons and movies; the difference with these three is they took it to the next level as they moved from childhood to adolescence.

In high school they became more mobile with the freedom and independence that a driver's license and borrowing your parent's car can bring. Now they were able to explore old graveyards, many times with Ouija boards, and investigate old abandoned houses in the woods because they looked scary, therefore must be haunted according to their train of thought and expectations. During this period, Lance Brown, the UPPRS tech manager and a childhood friend from elementary school, started joining the nocturnal exploits with the original trio. They had their fair share of frightening experiences in their formative years as paranormal investigators. Some of these experiences were perceived, some fabricated by others, and some appeared to be authentic, and at the time frightening, paranormal events.

The first "haunted" target of the teenage paranormal explorers was an old, abandoned schoolhouse that had sat empty for many years. There was no paranormal history or local legends attached to the building, but it was old and foreboding in appearance, and therefore needed to be investigated. The group made multiple trips to the schoolhouse before finding a ladder that led to the attic. "That must be where the ghosts are," they decided. They wouldn't find out, however, as none of them could agree who would climb the ladder first.

On another cold and dark fall evening, they returned to the schoolhouse and with much false bravado told themselves they would make it to the attic. They didn't. Shortly after entering the house they heard screaming and footsteps coming down the stairs towards their location. After quickly assessing the situation, they did what any normal teenager would do in that situation: they ran like hell! As they rushed out the front door, the would-be investigators heard strange noises following behind them. Was that laughter? When they took a breath, glancing back to see what nefarious entity was surely in pursuit of their very souls, they saw three figures exiting the schoolhouse... dressed in white sheets with eyeholes cut out! Tim's two older brothers and one of their girlfriends, knowing the plans of their little brother and his crew, decided to set a Casper-the-Friendly-Ghost-like ambush, and it worked to perfection! As a group, this was their first taste of the adrenaline rush that fear can deliver, even if it was just a practical joke.

The foursome of Brad, Lance, Steve, and Tim soon found another abandoned house ripe for exploration. This one was farther outside of city limits and deeper in the woods; think Blair Witch the movie. This house definitely had an ominous feel to it and one night provided the group another terrifying encounter. As they made their way through the upper story, there was a loud bang on the wall and menacing yells coming from one of the bedroom closets. The team didn't know if it was something demonic or a mentally unstable homeless person, but being consistent in their methodology, they followed the same game plan from their previous exploits. They ran like hell! This time it turned out to be

Brad's older brother and some of his friends lying in wait and the loud crash was a baseball bat being slammed into the wall—we might add very close to Brad's head. So, one lesson the group learned very early, even before they became the UPPRS: do not tell people your locations pre-investigation. You just never know who might show up!

As their paranormal formative years continued, they did experience some truly terrifying events. One outing they will always remember occurred on a Devils Night in the early 1990s. The setting was an old cemetery in the country on a seldom used dirt road; the perfect location for a scary story. They found a tombstone near the back of the cemetery near the tree line, and armed with a Ouija board, they made an attempt to contact the dead. To their surprise, the board started to communicate with them. The group members individually denied it was their efforts causing the planchette to move. When asked whom they were speaking to, the board started to spell out a name: W A G... As the group looked down, they noticed for the first time that the name on the tombstone they were currently utilizing as a table started with a W A G. Without hesitation they collectively removed their hands, breaking communication. As they looked at each other, frozen in astonishment, excitement, and most of all fear, they heard a disembodied moan coming from the woods directly behind them. The brave foursome was experiencing their first unexplained paranormal event together and they did what they knew best. They ran like hell!

The guys went their own ways following high school; going to college, beginning careers, and starting families. Their friendship always remained intact, even as distance and the priorities of life became obstacles.

Tim went to Central Michigan University and earned his Bachelor of Arts in Communications. This afforded him the opportunity to move back home to the Sault and land a job in radio using his God-given talent, his voice. Combining his love of radio and the paranormal, he came up with an idea for a Halloween radio promotion to do a live ghost hunt on the air. Steve recalls, "I still vividly remember receiving an email from Tim in the fall of 2000 asking if I would like the opportunity to do a ghost hunt in a reportedly haunted house live on the air for a radio show. This was a chance for us to do what we've been doing since we were young kids and teenagers in high school, but now as an adult. My response to Tim's email was, 'Hell, yeah'." The radio station ran ads for listeners to call in with their ghost stories and a house would be chosen for the live on-air investigation from those submissions.

Sault Ste. Marie is the oldest city in Michigan, and among the oldest cities in the United States, so finding an historical home with a ghost story is never an issue. Dozens of candidates submitted stories and one was chosen based on their ghostly experiences as well as incredible photographic evidence they presented. The picture they submitted shows the exterior of the back of the house. Standing in an upstairs bedroom window is what appears to be a little boy, but at the time the photograph was taken no one was inside the house. The picture was clear enough to make out the shirt the boy was wearing, and the homeowners reported that nothing in the wardrobe of their son, close to the same age of the boy in the picture, matched that particular shirt. The family also reported traditional haunting activity such as items disappearing and showing up in strange locations without explanation and a closet door that would always open on its own no matter how secure it was when shut. This family and their story had everything they wanted for their first case.

Going into the first investigation, it's safe to say they were nervous and a little intimidated. Yes, this group had been into the paranormal all their lives, but this was the first time they'd ever investigated in front of other people, let alone homeowners looking for answers to the unexplained ordeal which they currently found themselves in. Throw in the fact their first-ever "official" investigation was part of a live Halloween radio broadcast and the pressure was on.

The group set out that night with limited equipment: several cameras, many rolls of film, VHS video cameras, and a cassette tape recorder, much of which was borrowed from friends and relatives. Lance didn't have much tech equipment to manage the first showing!

Research methods which had been garnered through years of studying the accounts and methodology of veterans in the paranormal field (Harry Price, Ed and Lorraine Warren, Dr. Hans Holzer, and many more) were about to come into play. This was a time prior to the onslaught of ghost hunting television programs, when reputable paranormal research groups were a scarce commodity. The guys conducted EVP sessions, set stationary cameras to cover the paranormal hot spots, including the bedroom window where the ghostly image of the boy was captured on film, used trigger objects in an attempt to lure out any lingering spirits, and investigated in pairs for both safety reasons and also to have two witnesses to possible phenomena. The team has since honed their skills and added thousands of dollars' worth of equipment, but basically they use the same techniques today, with the exception of running away from suspected paranormal activity. For better or worse, they now run towards it!

Throughout the night, the team heard the sound of a door opening and closing; not a paranormal occurrence, but friends of the family coming and going, excited to gawk at the "ghost hunters" as they conducted the late-night investigation/radio broadcast. One of the favorite memories of this night involved a soundboard engineer from the radio station who was attempting to immerse himself in the ghost hunt. He was standing in the middle of the kitchen when he excitedly reported that he was feeling a cold spot around him which was isolated to his current position. Brad was quick to point out, "That's because you're standing under a ceiling fan, dumbass," a perfect example of displaying debunking skills since day one!

The team occupied the home until 6 AM, pleasantly surprised by the hospitality of the homeowners. "I mean, who are we, just some guys calling ourselves paranormal investigators with no track record or real-world experience on our resume. They welcomed us into their home like we were old friends," remembers Steve. "This was a typical October night in the Upper Peninsula, so it was cold, dark and rainy. They had chili and hot apple cider ready for us, which was much appreciated.

"This hospitality is something that continued throughout the years and still does today, which never ceases to amaze us. People will open their homes and their personal lives to us. Business owners will hand us the keys to their establishments without hesitation. This level of responsibility and trust is not lost on us and is something we do not take for granted. Our team name and the impression we leave on people is of great value to us and hopefully we have reciprocated the kindliness and respect presented to us. We strive to make sure no matter what environment we're investigating, it looks the same way at the end of the night, or in a lot of cases early morning, as it did when we began."

Over the years, additional members have joined the team. The common factor with all new additions remained consistent with their origins: friends that share a common interest in the paranormal. Each new prospect was a friend of at least one, but usually multiple team members of the UPPRS before being voted in as an official part of the team. Jason Fegan, Matt Barr, Matty McLeod, Ryan "Hillbilly" McLeod, and Michelle Carrick have all become integral parts of the UPPRS family and each brings a unique set of skills, perspectives and life experiences to their mission.

The UPPRS team. From left to right, front row: Jason Fegan, Matt Barr; middle row: Lance Brown, Ryan McLeod, Tim Ellis; back row: Brad Blair, Steve LaPlaunt, Matt McLeod.

Most team members were born and raised in the Upper Peninsula, Ryan being the team's only "troll." For those not familiar with Michigan vernacular, people living in the U.P. are known as Yoopers and those inhabiting the Lower Peninsula, south of the Mackinaw Bridge, (hence, living under a bridge), are affectionately known as trolls.

So what sets the UPPRS apart from other paranormal groups of the day? "We have seen many paranormal teams and individuals come and go throughout our 20 years of existence, while we have remained an intact and functioning group of paranormal enthusiasts," says Steve. "We're not prescribing a cookbook for how to establish a sustainable group in this field, but for us it worked."

Tim adds, "This group of individuals with a shared interest had the initiative, drive, and means to take a love of all things creepy to the next level. We're not just a team, but also a paranormal family. Not just another group wearing black t-shirts calling ourselves ghost hunters, but first and foremost, we are friends. We have shared ghostly encounters, terrifying unexplained events, and more than a few laughs, but most importantly, all have been memorable moments together."

The Upper Peninsula Paranormal Research Society has had the privilege of investigating some amazing locations, meeting remarkable individuals, and experiencing first-hand what can happen when the unseen world intrudes on the everyday lives of normal people. The following stories are taken from select case files of actual paranormal investigations. So settle in, get comfortable, and join the UPPRS as they take you along on their journey through the supernatural!

Whitefish Point Lighthouse and the Great Lakes Shipwreck Museum

"WE'RE HOLDING OUR OWN."

On a gale-ridden November night in 1975, these would be the final words transmitted from the SS *Edmund Fitzgerald* before it disappeared into the autumn storm, carrying all 29 crew members to the bottom of Lake Superior. Although the *Fitzgerald* would be the largest ship to falter in Lake Superior, or any of the five Great Lakes for that matter, it is far from the only vessel to claim the lives of seaworthy mariners off a stretch of land known as the Shipwreck Coast; their final visage being a glimmer of light shining from the distant beacon of the Whitefish Point light tower, seeming to offer hope to the doomed crews.

Victims of these shipwrecks may well haunt the shores at Whitefish Point, as reports of phantom sailors and sightings of ghost ships in the waters off its rocky coastline have been reported by both visitors and employees at the point for many years. However, the spectral encounters are far from limited to those who perished in the

1

lake. Other ghostly figures spotted on the lighthouse grounds include a young girl in historical period dress who is seen inside numerous buildings, a Native American woman said to roam the nearby woods, a young lady wearing what appears to be 1800s clothing gazing out from the light tower galley, and a man in a dark blue light keeper's uniform, who checks in on the guests of the bed and breakfast currently operated in the U.S. Coast Guard Crew Quarters building, former home to the Whitefish Point Lifeboat Rescue Station.

The history of the area now called Whitefish Point predates European settlers by many centuries. Some anthropologists believe early Native Americans had established a fishing camp at the point as far back as 20,000 years. However long ago it may have been, the piece of land jutting out into what the Ojibwe called Gichi-Gami, or "Great Sea," now known as Lake Superior, served as a source of sustenance for the tribal people during the summer months for many years. When autumn arrived, they would abandon this camp and move inland to the shelter of the forest, which provided some protection from the harsh elements of the northern winters.

Although the first European explorers and voyageurs arrived in this part of the country in the early 1600s, there would be no permanent white settlers in the region until the 1870s. The winters were too rough and the area too remote for a dependable supply route to be established between the point and nearest communities.

Even with a steady flow of settlers arriving in the Upper Peninsula, the region was still quiet in winter, but warmer months had become something entirely different. In the 1930s, commercial fishermen, having learned of the abundant catches brought in by the natives of the area, began establishing full-scale fishing operations at the point. With commercial shipping on Lake Superior increasing at a rapid pace, it was easy to package barrels of salted fish to send along to larger communities to be sold at a handsome profit. The opportunity for employment in the fisheries attracted men seeking work, many of whom would relocate their families to an area south of the point, which would eventually become known as the village of Paradise, Michigan.

The ever-expanding number of commercial vessels on this largest of the Great Lakes brought business opportunities previously unavailable to the communities that dotted its shoreline, but often at great cost to the many men who worked aboard these ships. Early shipping could be a treacherous venture on any of the lakes; however, Lake Superior had its own special perils, and the shoreline running from Whitefish Point to the west for 40 miles was one of them. This stretch, which came to be known as the Shipwreck Coast, is possibly the most dangerous area in all of the Great Lakes. With varying depths and a lack of bay areas to run to when the seas turned rough, this route claimed many ships and sailors over the years, with the first commercial wreck occurring in November of 1816; a ship ironically named *The Invincible*.

The UPPRS Team at Whitefish Point Lighthouse. Left to right: Brad Blair, Lance Brown, Tim Ellis, Jason Fegan, Steve LaPlaunt, Matt Barr, Michelle Carrick, Ryan McLeod. Credit: Don Hermanson.

3

The increasing importance of this maritime trade route was not lost on the United States government. In 1847, Congress approved the construction of a lighthouse at Whitefish Point to aid in early navigation. The original structure, built of brick and stone, went into service during the 1849 shipping season. The first light keeper assigned the duty of running the Whitefish Point Lighthouse was James A. Starr, who resigned prior to ever taking his post. Conditions at the point may have improved over the years; however, it was still a remote area offering few comforts and little contact with the outside world. The man who actually became the first keeper, James VanRenselaer, manned the light from May of 1849 through May of 1851 when he too resigned the post. Although the position was seasonal, the remoteness of the area could make it unbearable.

During the first 20 years of operation, light keepers came and went, normally resigning within a year or two of their appointment, not wishing to endure the conditions of this secluded outpost any longer than necessary. Another major issue was the lighthouse itself: the stone structure was no match for the intense Lake Superior storms and had begun to deteriorate into a state of disrepair. The light station might have been left to crumble into obscurity and the point to return to its natural, forested state had it not been for a seemingly unlikely ally: President Abraham Lincoln.

With the Civil War raging, the need for raw materials to produce weapons and ammunition was critical. Much of the iron ore supplied to Union factories was mined in the Lake Superior region and was transported by ship to refineries located along the shores of the lower lakes. Fearing a possible disruption in shipping, President Lincoln authorized construction of a new iron tower, which could better withstand the fury of a Lake Superior storm. The new light tower, along with a then-modern keeper's quarters, went into full service in 1862, and is still operational today (although the keeper's quarters are now operated as part of a museum, and no longer require a full-time resident).

Even with the welcoming glow of the beacon shining across the lake, many ships and their crews never reached the shelter and relative security of Whitefish Bay. In 1876, just west in nearby Vermillion, a

Lifesaving Station was established to aid distressed crews during storms and other emergencies. The men of the Lifesaving Service needed nerves of steel to attempt the daring rescues that could often end in disaster. Their mission was clear: row out into the lake and attempt to save any crew and passengers of a disabled or doomed ship. The Service hoped you yourself would return safely, but that was not a requirement of the job; risking life and limb was. They definitely earned their pay; in the 23-year period spanning 1890 through 1913, there were a recorded 32 wrecks on the Shipwreck Coast, the men of the Vermillion station responsible to dispatch aid to them all.

The Lifesaving Service performed death-defying acts of bravery from the Vermillion station until 1944, when navigational technologies rendered the service obsolete. Still, even with the best surfmen operating out of the station, many lives were lost in late fall storms, the dreaded Gales of November, taking ships' crews to the bottom of Superior. In the colder months, the bodies of these unfortunate mariners often became encased in ice, and floated to the shore during the spring thaw, to be chopped out of the ice and buried in unmarked graves in the dunes that run along the Lake Superior coast.

One of the earliest ghost stories at the point centers around one such unfortunate soul. A sign displayed in the Surfboat House, now a part of the Great Lakes Shipwreck Museum complex, tells the tale of Three Fingers Riley, a shipwreck victim who was found frozen in the lake. When the surfman who discovered him began using a hatchet to chop Riley's corpse from its casket of ice, he accidentally severed an index finger from the body. Legend has it that the restless spirit of the sailor now walks the lonely shore in search of his missing finger, reaching out a bloody hand to snatch up anyone unfortunate enough to be wandering the beach alone. Although this story is believed to have been invented by members of the Lifesaving Service to frighten rookie surfmen, there is record of a surfman using an axe to chop a body from the ice. The victim's name: William Riley!

Another of the spirits said to haunt Whitefish Point is that of a young girl who died tragically on the property. In 1921, the United States Navy established a radioman-in-charge position at the point, an occupation that over the years became obsolete but was crucial to early naval operations of that time. One evening while entertaining company, the radioman and his wife heard a loud commotion from the upstairs of their home. Their two young daughters had been playing with a lantern and accidentally caught fire to a portion of the second floor. Although the older daughter managed to escape the blaze, the younger girl was not so lucky, and later died from the injuries she sustained. In 1927, new living quarters were constructed for the family of the radioman. These newer quarters still exist at the point, and today are utilized by the Great Lakes Shipwreck Museum, a theater operated on the ground floor with guest quarters on the second level.

One evening, a visitor was filming the grounds and various structures that make up the Great Lakes Shipwreck Museum campus when he caught what appeared to be the head and upper torso of a young child looking out from the second floor of the theater building, the former housing for the family of the radioman. The figure was captured on his camera moving from one window to the next in a seemingly curious manner. The following day, the cameraman chatted with a staff member assigned to the theater, asking who lived in the upper quarters. The puzzled employee assured him the building had been empty the previous evening and, furthermore, no one had been in the upper level for several days.

Various visitors have reported seeing a young girl who appeared dressed for a historical reenactment. As no such program is offered by the museum, the workers became perplexed. Could these people have all encountered the same spirit; and could it be a young girl from the 1920s, playing on the grounds of her eternal childhood home?

No lighthouse history is complete without tales of a phantom light keeper, and Whitefish Point is no exception. Though the light is now automated and overseen from 73 miles away by the U.S. Coast Guard's Sault Ste. Marie, Michigan base, it housed a resident light keeper for a full century, from 1848 through 1947. Many men have lived through trying times and tense situations in their role as master of the light; however, the person most suspect to be remaining at this station is the man who held the title of Head Light Keeper the longest, Keeper Robert Carlson.

Robert Carlson didn't come to his position at Whitefish Point by the normal means of being assigned the role, but rather took charge through a "trade" with his predecessor, Captain Charles Kimball. In 1902, Carlson was light keeper of the Marquette Harbor Light Station, another Lake Superior lighthouse located 150 miles west of Whitefish. Keeper Kimball had high school-aged children and wished for them to carry on their education, something not possible in the remote area in which they currently lived. He suggested to Carlson that they swap assignments, Carlson taking control of the Whitefish station and Kimball moving to Marquette, enticing him with the prospect of earning a higher wage, as the keeper at Whitefish was also assigned the responsibility of making reports for the U.S. Weather Station at Whitefish Point, a task which would pay an extra $10 per month. Whether it was the extra money or just a much wanted change of scenery, Carlson agreed to the swap, and in 1902 he moved his wife and three children to the remote outpost at the point.

The Finnish-born Carlson had started working for the Lighthouse Service in 1885, and after moving over from Marquette, spent the bulk of his career, a full 28 years, at Whitefish Point. These turned out to be significant years for his normally quiet new homestead. During the period of Prohibition, it was commonplace for smugglers to run boatloads of Canadian booze across the lake to the Whitefish area, using the light from the station to guide their way to the American coast, where it could be easily transported to more populated areas and sold at a hefty profit. Although not a part of his regular duties, Carlson was expected to keep an eye out for these traffickers and report any suspicious activities to the authorities at Sault Ste. Marie. Smugglers, however, were far from the major concern to face the area, as Whitefish would also become a location of great military significance during the height of World War I.

As during the Civil War, the military relied on shipments of iron ore from the mines near Lake Superior for the production of vehicles and artillery needed in the war effort, and the German government was intent to disrupt this supply chain. One summer during this period, a new assistant keeper and his wife arrived at the point. Despite being in such a secluded location, the assistant keeper tended to shy away from Carlson and his family, he and his wife operating in an almost secretive fashion. After a lengthy period of this awkward, often standoffish behavior, Carlson became suspicious. He noticed that not only were the assistant and his wife avoiding any unnecessary contact with him but also were paying great attention to the daily freighter traffic, making note of the dates and times ships would pass the point. After observing this behavior for a period of time, Carlson confronted the assistant and questioned him on his motives. As it turned out, his suspicions were justified; the two were German spies, planted at the point to discern a shipping routine that an attack plan could be based on. The assistant panicked and attacked Carlson, splitting his head open with a blunt object before rushing away from the scene. Carlson immediately ran into the lighthouse, delaying medical attention, and sent a communication to the nearest law enforcement, which at the time was 73 miles away in Sault Ste. Marie. A contingency of government agents arrived by boat, shackling the couple and removing them to be imprisoned until the end of the war. Plans that could have ended with a German attack on American trade routes had been foiled; Keeper Robert Carlson was a hero.

Carlson served the remainder of his career at the Whitefish Point station, raising not only his children but also two grandchildren in his home beneath Lake Superior's oldest beacon. He retired after 40 years of service to Sault Ste. Marie in 1931, where he lived out his remaining years, passing in 1939.

Several others held the title of Head Keeper following Carlson, up until 1947 when the Coast Guard assigned a crew of six to oversee all operations at the point. The beacon became automated in 1970, eliminating the need for any full-time staff, returning the area to a quiet solitude it hadn't known since the lighthouse had been built.

Aside from regular visits by Coast Guard personnel and the occasional sightseer, Whitefish Point remained fairly stagnant, its structures once again falling into disrepair, until 1983 when the Great Lakes Shipwreck Historical Society reached an agreement with the Coast Guard to establish a museum complex at the point, and breathe new life into the remaining historic structures.

Although no living person has held the title of lightkeeper since 1947, many people, staff and visitors alike, have reported run-ins with a man both acting and dressing the part. The most dramatic of these encounters seem to take place in the former Coast Guard Crew Quarters, now operated as a seasonal bed and breakfast by the Shipwreck Society. Guests have reported waking to the sound of doorknobs being turned, disembodied footsteps pacing the halls, and even run-ins with a man in a dark blue suit resembling a lightkeeper's uniform.

One evening, a maintenance employee who had worked late decided that, rather than risk driving home down the dark, rural stretch of road, which would present the risk of collision with deer, bear, moose, or other forest dwellers, he would spend the night in one of the unoccupied rooms of the crew quarters. He had heard stories over the years of the supposed phantoms who wandered the grounds at night, but being very skeptical, he had always brushed them off as simply the wild imaginations of tourists who were unfamiliar with the natural sounds emanating from the forest or the winds moaning across the lake. He had never encountered anything to give credence to these tales, and they definitely would not keep him from getting some rest after a long day of working overtime hours to get the buildings ready for the cold winter months ahead.

Settling into a vacant room, he hoped to catch a few hours of sleep before the sunrise, making his drive home less treacherous. He was fortunate to be working during the "off season," when the building was closed to overnight visitors for the year. He had his pick of rooms and did not have to worry about being bothered by the comings and goings of other guests. Shortly after dozing off, he was startled awake by the sound of the doorknob turning and the light flicking on. Thinking it was another employee coming to rouse him, he grudgingly rolled over to find himself alone in the room. Confused, but still exhausted from his long day's work, he got up, checked the hall, switched off the light, and returned to bed. No sooner had he pulled up the covers when the light switched back on! Becoming more unnerved by this strange occurrence, he once again rose from the bed to put out the light. As he walked toward the switch, which refused to remain in the off position, he was greeted by the sound of footsteps approaching his door. Thinking this may all have been an elaborate joke by another employee who he would now catch in the act, he quickly flung open the door to reveal...an empty hallway. This proved more than even a hardcore skeptic like himself could take. Roadway hazards or not, he was not spending another minute in that room! Nor would he plan on working any more late shifts at the point, and definitely none that would find him there by himself after dark.

The UPPRS team had heard stories over the years of these purported hauntings at Whitefish; after all, with the lighthouse and Great Lakes Shipwreck Museum being among the top tourist destinations in the Upper Peninsula, these stories tended to spread far and wide. The Yoopers team had been contacted by a woman who claimed she had witnessed a large freighter, resembling the *Edmund Fitzgerald,* traveling toward the point, only to disappear into a fog bank. When the fog lifted, the ship was gone as well, seemingly vanishing into the morning horizon. This was far from the first ghost ship reported off the point. In the early 1900s, Keeper Carlson reported seeing an old-fashioned freighter canoe, the kind used by early Native Americans and French voyageurs, washed ashore. When he ventured out to check on the seemingly abandoned boat, it was gone, never to be seen again. Tales of phantom ships moving silently through the waters of Superior had indeed become almost commonplace.

The call that would bring the team to investigate the purported paranormal activity of the point came from another witness, a filmmaker from upper Michigan's Keweenaw Peninsula named Don Hermanson, who produced documentaries on unique historical locations. Don was the visitor who had filmed what he believed to be the young child in the second story windows of the theater building. He was eager to have his footage reviewed by the team and was intent to discover more of the ghost lore of the point.

The next time the team heard from Don, it was with surprising news: "I spoke to the director of the Shipwreck Society that runs Whitefish Point. He'd love to have you guys come out to investigate the property, and if you decide to go, I'd like to tag along and film the investigation for an upcoming project." Although some team members were apprehensive about having an outsider film an investigation

("What if he edits footage and turns our words around to try making us look ridiculous?"), the chance to investigate such an iconic landmark couldn't be passed up, and plans were set in motion.

It was a late-summer evening when the investigation took place. As the team emerged from the long stretch of tree-lined road that brought them to the point, the scene that greeted them was anything but foreboding: a lengthy view of pristine Lake Superior shoreline meeting the dense foliage of northern Michigan wilderness. Not hard to understand why some people refer to this area as God's Country.

Immediately, the Yoopers took to unloading the vanload of equipment and beginning set up. This was their largest investigation to date, and all tools at their disposal were needed to cover four buildings and the grounds of the campus. Unfortunately, the old crew quarters, which the ghost in the light keeper's uniform seemed so drawn to, had guests for the night and were off limits, but with the daunting task of running a thorough investigation of the keeper's quarters, Great Lakes Shipwreck Museum, gift shop, and theater building ahead of them, one less structure would ease what was sure to be an intense night.

For rookie investigator Ryan McLeod, this was his first full scale investigation with the team. "There's so much more to setting up for an investigation than I'd imagined; figuring camera angles, taping down cords, taking base readings…I guess we don't just go lights out and dive in!" Ryan observed.

"Not quite," said Lance Brown, head of the tech department. "On a job this size, it'd be easy to spend as much time on setup as investigating."

Last but not least, once all the wires were run and cameras adjusted, in came the food: crock pots full of chili and con queso, sandwich trays, bags of chips and snack mixes filled an entire table. It would be a long night of investigating, and this team was not doing it on empty stomachs! When Don Hermanson arrived to film the investigation, he was almost as impressed by the buffet as by the team's tech setup. "Do you guys eat like this on every investigation?" asked Don.

"Yeah, do we?" asked Ryan.

The guys laughed. They all knew it was a long night ahead, but this was a bit excessive even by heavyweight standards.

"Guess we may have overdone it a bit," said Steve LaPlaunt.

"Oh yeah? Let's see what's left at the end of the night!" replied Jason Fegan.

One more visitor joined the team that night. Maritime historian and author Fred Stonehouse had asked to tag along on the investigation in order to write an article for a magazine he regularly contributed to, the focus of which would be the ghost lore of Whitefish Point and the UPPRS handling of a paranormal investigation. Although running late due to fighting off a case of food poisoning, Fred appeared energized and excited for the long night ahead.

After joining in on the pre-investigation dinner, Stonehouse sat down at the makeshift team headquarters with Tim Ellis for a run through of the group's methods and procedures, receiving a quick tutorial before joining in on the night's activities. Once he was brought up to speed, Fred compared the UPPRS' investigating methods to deer hunting: setting up the equipment and trigger objects (specific items which may attract a spirit) were his equivalent of prepping a blind and laying out bait for the deer. Sitting back and monitoring the cameras for a period was much like sitting in the deer blind; watching, listening… waiting for that one golden moment to arrive. Leave it to a Yooper to compare researching the paranormal to hunting wild game!

With fully charged gear and full stomachs, it was time for the team to begin their investigation. Cameras had been recording and monitored for roughly a half hour, just enough time to discern any possible visual contaminations due to dust from forced air heat or lights bouncing back from reflective surfaces, which may cause false assumptions of paranormal activity. The team would now break off into smaller groups and begin what was sure to be a long, and hopefully active, night of investigating.

Ryan and Lance started the night in the keeper's quarters. Decorated with the furnishings of an early 1900s home and accented with maritime antiques, the house has a certain charm, but also an undeniable creep factor, mainly due to four very life-like mannequins displayed throughout the building. Maintenance workers had reported hearing phantom voices and footsteps in this house on many occasions, so this location would be a focal point throughout the night.

As the two entered, all was quiet. Lance turned on his EMF meter, used to measure the level of electromagnetic energy in an area, often theorized to be the lifeblood of paranormal manifestations. Ryan followed, his first time in this building, armed with an ambient thermometer, watching for sudden variances in temperature. They began by confirming the earlier base readings of EMF and temperatures through the lower level. As they rounded a corner into the kitchen, Ryan jumped! Just steps away stood an old woman, long grey hair pulled back in a bun and holding a rolling pin, glaring at him! He froze for a second before hearing the sound of Lance chuckling. With a deep exhale, Ryan realized the mannequins of the house had scored their first scare of the night. "Damn creepy things," he mumbled.

As the duo made their way into the next area, a living room decorated with period furnishings, an antique Victrola, and, yes, another mannequin, Lance's gaze locked on his EMF meter. Before he could say a word, Ryan shouted, "Hey! The temperature in here just dropped four degrees."

"The EMF levels just spiked as well," replied Lance.

As they looked up from their instruments, what appeared to be a dark shadow quickly moved across the room and darted down the empty hallway. The two gave chase, following the figure up the stairs to the second floor where they discovered...dead silence. No shadowy movement in any of the rooms, no fluctuations on the meters; the figure had vanished. They barely had time to process what had just happened when their two-way radio crackled to life, Tim's voice instructing: "All right guys, let's wrap up this rotation and meet back at headquarters to compare notes." They headed out of the building, feeling the rush of adrenaline that tends to accompany such an encounter, and eager to learn what the rest of the team had experienced so far. After all, the night had just begun!

As the team reassembled in their makeshift headquarters on the second floor of the gift shop building, reports from the first stage of the night were exchanged. Tim and Michelle Carrick, the team's other rookie member, had been in the theatre building where all was quiet. Jason and Matt Barr, accompanied by Fred, had just returned from the museum where they reported hearing a faint whisper, too soft to make out any distinct words, yet clearly feminine. Steve and Brad Blair, along with Don, were the last to return. They had been on the lakeshore attempting an EVP (electronic voice phenomenon) session in the hopes of communicating with one of the many doomed sailors who had perished off the point. Unfortunately, as can often occur when investigating outdoors, the sounds of nature and the winds coming off Lake Superior made these recordings inaudible. Don didn't seem to mind though, as he exclaimed jokingly in his thick Yooper accent, "That Brad really knows how to talk to them ghosts, eh?" which brought a good laugh to the team, now into their second round at the buffet table.

With Ryan and Lance clearly the winners of Best Experience in the first rotation, and stomachs once again full, it was time to split up and head back out into the night.

After a couple quiet rotations with nothing eventful being reported, the smaller groups were re-shuffled in an effort to mix perspectives, as it was only nearing the halfway point, and a long night of investigating lay ahead.

As Tim and Steve trekked down the path to the theater, Don came hurrying behind. "That's the building where I saw the kid in the upstairs window. I'm coming with you guys!"

They began an extensive EVP session, attempting to contact whomever it may have been that Don had the previous encounter with. After a lengthy, and unfortunately quiet, attempt to speak with the spirit in the theater, they had begun to gather their gear and exit the building when suddenly they all froze: from the vacant second story came the

Brad Blair taking readings at the Whitefish Point Lighthouse Gift Shop.
Credit: Don Hermanson.

distinct sound of footsteps on the wooden floor. Don hurriedly started his camera as Tim and Steve made their way up the narrow staircase, both apprehensive and excited to find out what waited for them upstairs. Entering the empty apartment, Tim began another session with his audio recorder. "Can we help you?" he asked to the seemingly empty room.

"Help…help," was the soft reply that came through the device, clearly a feminine voice.

They continued the session, but no further communications were relayed, and the theater once again fell silent. Time to head back to base and see how the other groups were faring.

As the trio exited the theater, ready to report their auditory experiences to the rest of the team, they were greeted by a very animated Jason and Michelle, who had just left the Shipwreck Museum, with a story of their own to tell.

"Dude, you're not going to believe what just happened," Jason exclaimed in an excited voice. "Something walked right by me! We were in the museum when I heard the 'swooshing' sound of clothing, almost like corduroy pantlegs rubbing against each other, and it walked right past me! I've never experienced anything like it before!"

The night's activity, it seemed, was starting to ramp up.

As the group reconnoitered at home base, exchanging stories of the past hour and further decimating their makeshift food court, Don reviewed his recording from the upstairs of the theater. Suddenly, his face lit up. Immediately following the "help" EVP recorded by Tim, another nearly inaudible, but distinctly female, voice was captured by his camera.

"It seems to be the same voice," said Tim. "I wish we could make out what she's saying. Considering the timing, it could easily be a continuation of the other EVP."

Unfortunately, the recorded phrase was not discernable, and the team was left to speculate on what the disembodied message may have been.

The next venture would find Brad and Matt in the keeper's quarters. The investigation was now into the later hours, and as tends to happen, the team was worn down and a bit stir crazy. Matt began cracking jokes, first chuckling about things that were happening during the investigation: the mountain of food; statements made by Don and Fred, who were unfamiliar with the field of paranormal research; Lance walking into the bathroom to the startling sound of a phantom toilet flush; and then zeroing in on the mannequins which had earlier given Ryan such a scare. As the guys carried on, they were suddenly startled by the realization that they weren't the only two laughing. From the second floor, they could clearly hear the giggling of what sounded like a small child. The jokes stopped as the hair rose on both their necks. Rushing up the stairs, the two found themselves in the room they believed the laughter had come from: a small nursery, complete with vintage baby carriage and creepy, threadbare dolls. Matt quickly set up an EMF detector as Brad turned on the audio recorder and started an EVP session. "Is anyone else in this room with us?"

The EMF meter jumped.

"Are you a boy?"

No response.

"A girl?"

Once again, the meter spiked.

"Is this your home?"

Another movement of the meter, which the guys believed to indicate an affirmative response. The questions continued over several minutes, with mixed responses, or lack thereof. When the meter had sat motionless over several inquiries, the questioning stopped, and it was time to play back the audio. As the two braced for what was sure to be a volley of answers and conversation from their new spectral friend, Brad pressed the play button on the recorder to reveal…dead silence. Not a single word or sound had been picked up during the entire exchange. The audio phenomena had occurred, the manipulation of the electromagnetic field had taken place, but whoever had joined them in the house was careful to keep their voice to themselves.

As night moved closer to morning, the last rotations drew blanks: no activity to report from any of the locations. Tim, exhausted from a long night's work, made the executive decision: "We'll all go together to the museum for one last session, then call it a night." None disagreed, as the long task of tearing down and packing the equipment would be time consuming, and the team had been working for better than eight hours.

The crew filed into the building, passing the polished brass bell that had been reclaimed from the wreck of the *Edmund Fitzgerald*, now the centerpiece of the museum. Everyone spread out among the displays of salvaged artifacts and maritime histories. Tim began the final EVP session of the night: "We want to thank you for allowing us to be with

17

you tonight. We are getting ready wrap things up, so if you can make your presence known to us in any way, we would greatly appreciate it." No sooner had the words left Tim's mouth than a crackling sound was heard in the corner. Brad quickly directed his camera in the direction of the noise and began snapping pictures. As Tim continued his session, Brad quickly reviewed his photos on the camera's monitor. Almost all the pictures revealed nothing more than the corner of the room where he had aimed the camera. All except one. The first picture contained something that appeared to be a large blue energy form. Upon closer examination, there were found to be two overlapping forms, resembling a conspicuous part of the human anatomy. When it was downloaded to the computer and viewed on a larger screen, there was no doubt: the UPPRS had been mooned by a ghost! Proof that the spirits had had enough of the team for one night, and that a sense of humor can last into the afterlife!

The team, worn out and more than ready to have the hour-plus drive home behind them, disassembled cameras, gathered up the equipment, threw their gear into hard-shelled cases and crammed tangled cables into totes in a manner which would guarantee a lecture from Lance in the near future. Packing up the leftovers was not a problem. As Jason had predicted at the beginning of the night, there was nothing left, just a messy table and a couple of empty crock pots.

With a memorable night behind them, the team pulled away from Whitefish Point, greeted by the first rays of the sunrise. There would be many hours of audio and video recordings to review before the case file could be finalized, but that would come after some much needed sleep.

THE ANTLERS RESTAURANT

When visiting the hometown of the Upper Peninsula Paranormal Research Society, Sault Ste. Marie, Michigan, there are countless things to see and do. One top-rated destination for locals and visitors alike is The Antlers Restaurant. Located at 804 E. Portage Avenue, it stands across the street from St. Mary's River, giving patrons an excellent view of the Great Lakes freighters either heading to or coming from, the world-famous Soo Locks.

When entering the dining area of The Antlers, most first-time visitors have to stop to take it all in. The walls and ceiling are adorned with over 200 taxidermy animals, along with artifacts from a time gone by. Visitors can look upon a pride of lions, a polar bear that stands at least seven feet tall, a giant snake making its way up one of the wooden beams, and possibly the crown jewel of the place, the ever elusive "jackalope." You will want to research that one! Every inch of the dining area has something to behold.

The menu is filled with fantastic fare from the region, such as all kinds of Great Lakes fish, especially whitefish, stews, the famous U.P. Pasty, and amazing burgers like the Paul Bunyan Burger, to name a few. Once settled at a table, patrons are encouraged to ask for The Antlers' "Bells and Whistles." Cover your ears and enjoy!

The dining experience at The Antlers is genuinely like no other, and you are highly encouraged to visit them for the first time or a return visit. Hundreds of visitors have shared stories of enjoying their time there and loving the food, but always having a feeling of being watched. That would be easy enough to write off considering a couple hundred animals around the room are watching them eat. But, is that the *only* reason they have this feeling? The history and lore of The Antlers are as rich and intriguing as the interior decorations that cover the walls. Perhaps it's much more than just the animals that are watching the visitors.

The history of the building dates back to before Prohibition. At one time the upstairs housed a location for men to visit the ladies of the night. During Prohibition, the business was known as the Bucket of Blood Saloon and Ice Cream Parlor. The saloon was said to have closed down, and a proper family-run ice cream parlor was in operation. Or so it seemed to those who did not know any better. The saloon relocated to the basement, and the movement of alcohol from Canada to the United States and into the basement of The Bucket of Blood was quite easy considering you can stare at the shores of Canada while enjoying a meal inside the current Antlers Restaurant. The disguise worked for a while until the government noticed that the finances submitted for the ice cream parlor showed $900 in sales each month, but only a gallon of ice cream was sold each month. The Feds eventually closed the joint down for running a speakeasy in the basement.

The years passed and eventually the place became what we know it as today. The business has seen several owners over the years, but the Kinney family held on to it the longest, passing it through generations. The last family of Kinneys to operate The Antlers was a brother and sister. The brother, Dan Kinney, was the one who first reached out to The UPPRS about coming in for an investigation. Knowing the history of this building and business, the team jumped at the opportunity to investigate.

The Antlers exotic dining room. Credit: Steve LaPlaunt.

The stars aligned for this first investigation of The Antlers on the team's annual Halloween radio broadcast, something they have done every year since 2000. To this day, on the night of October 30—

the team's anniversary—an investigation can be heard live on WUPN, Eagle 95.1, from an undisclosed location. But the fun didn't stop there at The Antlers. The team was accompanied by Director and Producer Don Hermanson, of Keweenaw Video Production Services. This investigation was the second of two for which Don followed the team, to be included on their first DVD release, *Ghost Hunting with the UPPRS*.

Preparation for the investigation began immediately. The team met with The Antlers' current and former employees to hear the ghostly tales of what went on in the building. The notes and stories continued to pile up; everyone who worked there had one or more stories to share. One episode spoke of an evening when all the customers had left and the employees had finished their cleaning. Five employees were sitting around chatting. One of them was new, and the others were sharing their ghost stories with her. Of course, as all good ghost stories need, this employee was a skeptic and laughed at the tales shared.

The night manager had left moments before, letting the wayward group know that all the lights were shut off, everything was unplugged, and she was locking the door behind her. After a few more stories were shared, the group stopped talking and stared at one another in disbelief. Where once only their voices and laughter filled the closed down business, now the building became filled with the sounds of a blaring jukebox. A jukebox that had recently been unplugged by the night manager!

The employees ran out of the office and into the main dining area where they were met with the blaring sounds of Jimi Hendrix ripping out the "Star Spangled Banner" coming from the jukebox! Instead of trying to make the music stop, the group quickly left the building and ran straight for the parking lot. There they stopped to catch their breath and try to figure out what had just happened. While they collected their thoughts, a loud thud came from the building's upstairs, which had been closed up and locked hours before. The sound seemed to come from the door leading outside to the parking lot where the group stood, as though someone, or something, was trying to get out. This was the last straw and enough for one night for this group of workers. They ran to their cars and left The Antlers in their rearview mirrors as quickly as their cars would take them.

Belly up to the bar at The Antlers. Credit: Steve LaPlaunt.

Another frightening event that a longtime and trusted night manager shared with the UPPRS is one that the team would not soon forget. The manager was closing up and the last to be in the building. She was ready to go home after a long night but still had a couple more things to finish up. While she put away some pots and pans, she heard a sound behind her and froze. When she finally turned around, there on the floor was a washtub that just moments ago sat securely on a shelf. The metal utensils it contained were now scattered all over the floor. Two other tubs on the shelf were untouched and sat perfectly in their positions.

Nerves now a bit raw, she started to clean up the newly formed mess when all of a sudden the feeling of being watched washed over her. She first brushed it away, telling herself it was her nerves heightened from the washtub incident. She tried to ignore the feeling of being watched, but she couldn't. She knew something was behind her. As she turned around, there it was! The head of a person peeking around the corner of the basement door, looking directly at her. But the head was near the ground, as though the person, or thing, was on all fours walking up the steps from the basement! Believing she was the only one still in the building, she screamed a sound straight from a Hollywood horror film. As the head slunk back toward the basement, she gathered enough nerve to check to see if perhaps an actual person was in the building with her and was heading back to the basement. As she approached the door to look down the stairs, no one was there!

The numerous other stories and events that have been shared run the gamut of hauntings, such as footsteps, voices, shadows, and invisible hands touching the workers. But one thing was for sure, years upon years of workers had come forward to share their stories, and the UPPRS was anxious to get in there and begin the investigation.

On the night of the annual Halloween broadcast with the radio station, the evening always has a little bit different feeling. Add to that the cameras and filming for the DVD, and the energy seemed a bit higher than usual. From the upstairs of the building, which used to house the brothel, to the farthest corner of the basement, which housed the speakeasy, and the main floor, which houses the restaurant, there was a lot of ground for the team to cover on this night. Between the size of the location, the radio team setting up, and the production team setting up, the preparation to start the night took longer than usual. By the time the location went dark and all equipment was up and running, The UPPRS was itching to get into the field and work.

The glitches, or unexplained electrical issues, began almost immediately. In one of the upstairs rooms, near the door where the five co-workers heard the big bang that sent them scattering for home, one of the team's cameras kept going in and out of focus and on and off the air. This had their Tech Team scratching their heads. The team's leader, Lance Brown, was unable to attend, leaving tech members Jason Fegan and Matt Barr to figure out what, or who, was messing with the gear. Although not wanting to give Lance the satisfaction of knowing they needed his help, Jason and Matt finally broke down and called him. Together the three tried to work out the issue. Then, for no particular reason, the problems stopped. Whatever was interfering with the camera was no more! Although the Tech Team will still to this day try and take credit for it, the rest of the team knows it was merely the ghosts done having their fun.

With all of that happening from the very beginning, the evening was already off to an exciting start. The Halloween broadcast rolled on and the production team kept filming. All of a sudden, everything amped up, as can be heard on the DVD.

"Wait, what happened?" asked Tim Ellis.

"We were touched," came across the voice of Steve LaPlaunt, faintly on the DVD and the radio show.

Team members Steve LaPlaunt and Ryan McLeod were coming from the kitchen area, wide-eyed and ready to share their story of what just happened. They were in the kitchen with another team member, Michelle Carrick, doing some work and conducting an EVP session. Steve and Ryan were standing next to each other. As cliché and classic as it sounds, the question was asked, "If someone is here, please give us a sign."

"I remember immediately thinking to myself, why is Ryan touching me?" said LaPlaunt. "As I turned to look at him and see what he wanted, he was staring directly at me and asked if I had just touched him! I said, 'NO, did you touch me?'"

McLeod answered with an emphatic, "NO!"

The two quickly realized they had been simultaneously touched immediately following the question for a sign to be given. "It felt like pressure followed by static electricity, if I had to put it into terms," said LaPlaunt. A physical touch, by invisible hands, correlated perfectly with what many past employees had experienced.

After that experience, as often happens on investigations, the energy of the night waned and activity slowed. The night ended with no other significant events. When the team sat down with the owners, they shared their personal experiences through the night, but unfortunately, the team's video and audio recorders were left void of any significant evidence. However, the team's personal experiences prompted them to request a return visit and an investigation of the restaurant, which the owners graciously and excitedly accepted.

A couple of months passed before the team could return, which made it the dead of winter and a cold night when the gear was once again hauled into The Antlers and set up for another full night of investigating. This time there was no radio show and no production company; it was only the team, focused and ready for another eventful evening. On this particular night, the group was accompanied by a psychic/medium with whom they had worked on a handful of investigations when they felt her services were needed. For the sake of anonymity, we will refer to her as Helen. Working with a psychic/medium is something the UPPRS takes very seriously, and they only work with those they know are accurate, ethical, and trusted in what they bring to a night in the field. The team always makes sure the person is never given prior information about the location and events of the site.

The night would start the opposite of their first visit there—slow! It seemed to be a night where the unseen residents were keeping to themselves. Then the footsteps started, first on the basement stairs and then through the main dining room. The team was alert, and the adrenaline was now flowing. The team quickly sent a group into the main dining area, joined by Helen, to conduct an EVP session and to see if they could make contact with whoever was walking. Helen quickly tapped into the energy, describing a long ago time when the building was filled with a lot of fun energy. "Happy and fun," Helen said. "He always wanted it to be happy and fun."

Some time went by before the group returned to headquarters. The audio recorder was quickly downloaded into the audio software, to begin listening back for possible communication. Team member Michelle Carrick was still relatively new to the team and it was time for her to learn how to listen to the audio and look for EVPs. Tim Ellis is the one who usually handles audio playback, so it was his job to teach Michelle how to use the program, what to look for in the sound waves, and what to listen for within the recordings.

"Okay, do you feel good about using this equipment?" asked Ellis.

"Yup, ready to take a crack at it, captain," replied Carrick.

H.Q. quickly filled with the sounds of, "Holy F#%$!" The entire team promptly looked at Michelle, who had jumped out of her seat and thrown the headphones to the ground. One hundred dollar headphones, at that!

"What in the hell is going on?" yelled team member Brad Blair. (As you can see, as the night goes on and events escalate, so does the language.)

"My name! Someone whispered my God-D%$# name to me in that recording," yelled Carrick, half laughing and at the same time on the verge of tears.

Ellis grabbed the headphones, first making sure the one hundred dollar pair of phones did not break, and then sat down to listen. He first brought the audio file back a couple minutes, then hit play and focused on the audio. Ellis heard Helen on the recording stating what she was seeing and feeling: "Happy and fun. He always wanted it to be 'MICHELLE' happy and fun." There it was! He heard it clear as day and looked up at Michelle.

She stared back with a look that asked, "Am I crazy, or not?"

"Oh my God," Ellis said, laughing and shocked at the same time.

"Why the hell are you laughing?" asked Carrick.

"Because this is friggin' amazing," said Ellis.

The team took turns listening and, every time, there it was. "Happy and fun. He always wanted it to be 'MICHELLE' happy and fun." Michelle's name was whispered right within Helen's talk, and this was her first time working EVP playback. What a baptism by fire for Michelle, hearing her very name whispered to her, as though the spirit knew she would be listening. It was a moment that the young ghost hunter, and the team, would never forget.

As the night went on, Helen kept hearing a name whispered to her. Pat was the name, and she couldn't figure out why. She kept telling the team to remember the name "Pat," and "cinnamon rolls." The team did as they were instructed and wrote down "Pat" and "cinnamon rolls." It was one of those events that would make sense later.

Eventually, it was time for the team to call it a night. Taking down the equipment is always the least favorite part of the night for the team. Mentally and physically drained, the last thing anyone on the team wants to do is walk around and pack up equipment, let alone pack it away nicely—another reason why the team is thankful for the Tech Team. Lance, Jason, and Matt Barr barked orders at the rest of the team to put the wires and gear away nicely. If it weren't for those three watching closely, the equipment would look like a five-year-old and a pack of puppies had packed the gear away.

While the paranormal teams are packing up and the gear is being shut down, unexpected personal experiences quite often can happen. Such an incident happened to team president, Tim Ellis.

"As I was walking down in the basement, I felt what I could best describe as walking through a spider web, but it didn't touch my face, it was the back of my neck," said Ellis. "I was by myself and walked through an archway. I quickly flinched and turned around; it felt like something was brushing or touching my neck. I first thought it had to have been a spider web. But after looking over the archway, there was nothing. Plus, we had walked through that same archway dozens of times that night. I knew no spider web was there, but I was trying to rationalize what had just touched my neck. Looking back on it now, I know what it was. I always knew what it was."

The post work of an investigation is always the most time-consuming. Hours upon hours of audio and video review can take days to complete. Plus, historical research might be needed to tie any loose ends from the night of the investigation. This particular investigation needed that historical research to try and figure out what Helen meant when she told the team to write down "Pat" and "cinnamon rolls."

28

"There is nothing more satisfying than when we do the post research and can tie it directly back to the investigation," said Blair, the team's Historian. "This was one of those times when it fits together like a puzzle."

More interviews with past employees revealed there was a woman named Pat who worked at The Antler. She was the restaurant's morning baker, famous for her cinnamon rolls. But, as far as the interviewees knew, she was still alive. They said she and her husband had moved after he retired. She hated to leave her job, but family out of state needed their assistance, so they packed up and moved away.

Blair went on to say, "At that point, I thought I had hit a dead end, but I wasn't ready to give up. And then one night, there it was! The obituary staring right back at me. Her name was Pat, and it spoke of her love for baking and how she was known for her cinnamon rolls, and how much she loved baking them when she worked for a restaurant in Sault Ste. Marie. It's one of those moments where you can almost put closure on an investigation."

Was Pat back where she loved to be, using Helen and the team to let that be known?

Whether you're a ghost enthusiast or someone looking for a good meal and fun experience, make sure The Antlers Restaurant is on your "To Do" list when visiting Sault Ste. Marie. And remember, while you're sitting there and feeling like you are being watched, it may be much more than the taxidermy cohorts sharing the room with you.

Seul Choix Point Lighthouse

A trip through Michigan's Upper Peninsula is always an adventure, whether you want it to be or not. After all, the main highways are two lanes from one end of God's Country to the other. Once you start to venture off those main roads, well, let's just say that's when the ghost stories come to life.

A two-hour trip southwest of the Upper Peninsula Paranormal Research Society's hometown of Sault Ste. Marie reveals one of these places. Most of the trip follows their two-lane highways across on M-28, a quick stroll down M-17 and then across on US-2. Following this route, you will end up in a small fishing village known as Gulliver, Michigan. It's one of those familiar U.P. towns, where if you blink, you could miss it. Once in Gulliver, the road trip takes a different view, turning onto Portland Road. The little bit of life you did see with other passing cars on the highway, no longer exists. The road narrows, the trees increase, and the distance between houses becomes farther and farther until the road turns into Seul Choix Road. At this point, if you are a first-time traveler, you start to wonder if you are indeed heading in the right direction. Could they possibly have made a terrible wrong turn somewhere? As the trees seem to close in on you, and you have asked yourself over and over if you should turn around, out of nowhere, you see it! Like a giant looking over the top of the trees stands the 77-foot light tower of the Seul Choix Point Lighthouse, welcoming you, or warning you. Either way, you have arrived.

The Guardians of The Great Lakes, Michigan, has more lighthouses dotting its shores than any other state; 129, to be exact. Seul Choix Point Lighthouse is one of those magnificent and haunted structures, sitting on the northern shore of Lake Michigan. Oh, and by the way, it's pronounced Sis Shwah Point Lighthouse. Do not pronounce it as it is spelled, or the locals immediately will know you are an out-of-towner. The name is French, meaning "only choice." This is how the early sailors referred to it, knowing it was the only choice of survival if you were caught in Lake Michigan during one of her epic storms. Sailors desperately searched for the light of Seul Choix and would take cover in her cove on the belly of the Upper Peninsula.

Established in 1892 and entirely constructed in 1895, Seul Choix Point Lighthouse over the years has no doubt saved the lives of countless sailors, but so too has it become the home of many spirits and ghostly tales, and the UPPRS had all intentions of getting to the bottom them.

The ghost stories and legends that surround Seul Choix are countless, with a handful of different spirits that are said to inhabit the old lighthouse. But of all the ghosts that call Seul Choix home, there is no argument over who is the most famous resident, and that is Captain John Joseph Willey Townshend.

Born in 1847 in Bristol, England, Townshend would end up working his entire life on the water. He worked his way up as a sailor stationed out of England, and then eventually found his way to Canada where he made his living as a fisherman. It is here that he married his first wife and started his family. When the fishing dried up in his area of Canada, Townshend and his family packed up and sailed for the United

States where they found their new home on Mackinac Island. Through the years, Townshend's career eventually found its way to the United States Lighthouse Services. Also during this time, he lost two wives. In 1901 Captain Joseph Willie Townshend was named the head lighthouse keeper of Seul Choix Point Lighthouse. Then, in 1904, Townshend married his third wife, Ruth Montgomery DuVall, who quickly and lovingly jumped into the role of mother and wife. Ruth kept a very tidy home, and one stringent rule she had was that Captain Townshend was not allowed to smoke his cigars, something he was very fond of, in the house.

On August 10th, 1910, at the age of 63, Captain Joseph Willie Townshend passed away after an eighteen-month ailment. Many believe it to be from gastritis. Whatever it was that Townshend suffered from, one thing is for sure, it was painful. Neighbors and friends tell stories of hearing him yelling and screaming from his upstairs bedroom. After his death, Captain Townshend was embalmed in the basement of the lighthouse and then laid for viewing in the parlor for days, while they waited for the family from out of town to arrive.

Now, almost 120 years later, Captain Townshend seems to still call Seul Choix Point Lighthouse his home! The stories and legends of the lighthouse have been shared and known in the region for many years. But it was in the early 2000s when the world would be introduced to Michigan's U.P.'s secret, thanks to a television show on Fox Family, later to become ABC Family, called *Scariest Places on Earth*. It was a television show that would take young, would-be ghost hunters, and put them in a reportedly haunted location armed with only POV cameras and their wits. Perhaps the scariest part of the entire television series was that it was hosted by Linda Blair, the possessed, pea-soup-spitting, owl-neck-spinning young girl of *The Exorcist*. And, if that was not creepy enough, it was narrated by the 1970s hippy spiritualist, with the *huge* sunglasses, from the original *Poltergeist*. Think, "Carol Anne, come to the light. Follow my voice and come to the light." Yeah, that lady! Played by Zelda Rubenstein. Overall, *Scariest Places on Earth.*was a well-produced show that was very popular for its time and brought Seul Choix Point Lighthouse to the forefront of all ghost-hunting enthusiasts.

Amid countless paranormal investigative teams reaching out to the Gulliver Historical Society, the entity that now runs and is responsible for the operations and upkeep of Seul Choix Point Lighthouse, the Upper Peninsula Paranormal Research Society was determined to get their own investigation going. After all, this was very early in the team's creation, and what a place this would be for them to sharpen their teeth and skills. It began with reaching out to Marilyn Fischer, the president of the Historical Society. After a couple emails and phone calls between Marilyn and the team's president, Tim Ellis, to his excitement, a date was set for the first of what would become many trips to the famous Seul Choix Point Lighthouse!

"I remember it like it was yesterday," said Ellis. "We had our monthly meeting at one of our local watering holes, something we are fond of doing." He laughed. "I couldn't wait to update and share with the team that we had been given the green light to have our night at Seul Choix."

The team quickly made preparations for their trip to Gulliver early that spring, which was still a couple months away. This was winter in the U.P. and waiting for spring is sometimes like waiting for paint to dry. Eventually spring came, and the team made their first road trip to the haunted lighthouse. The twelve-passenger van was loaded to the brim with equipment and eager UPPRS members. As the group traveled, the chatter was nonstop, and the excitement continued to grow.

"I even remember that we made a road trip CD for this particular night," recounted team member Jason Fegan. "Each of us chose two songs, and we ripped them to a CD. Ah, the good ol' days of ripping CDs."

The trip there seemed extremely fast as the team was lost in talk, music, laughter, and excitement for the night ahead. However, as chatter-filled as the van was, it soon became quiet the moment the tower of the lighthouse appeared over the treetops and loomed down on the young team. Eyes wide, some mouths open as well, the team just stared as they got closer to the famous structure that until this moment they had only read about.

"Surreal," said team member Steve LaPlaunt.

Surreal was really the only way to put it. Seul Choix was right in front of us, and it was time to do what we had gone there to do.

As the team got out of the van and unpacked the gear, they were greeted by Marilyn Fischer and a couple other members of the Gulliver Historical Society. The connection between Marilyn and the team was instant.

"It was like meeting one of our member's mother for the first time and introducing her to the team," recalls Brad Blair. "It was the start of an immediate friendship that has lasted through the years. We have given her every reason to trust us, and she does."

As the team continued to unload gear and to get ready for the first tour of the lighthouse, this was just the beginning of an amazing night for the UPPRS and their love affair with Seul Choix Point Lighthouse.

The moment you walk into the historical lighthouse you are immediately greeted with the overpowering sense of history. The smells, the look, and the feel scream years of memories and stories, and those stories were shared by Marilyn the moment the team walked in the door. The tales were countless. We saw where Captain Townshend laid in rest while friends and family visited after his passing. The stairwell where the footsteps of someone walking with the hard knock of boots on the wooden stairs, or on the metal stairs leading to the light, just like the kind of boots a lighthouse keeper would wear—but no one is ever there.

We were shown the kitchen table, an original piece found in the basement when renovations began and later was found disassembled and scattered to the four corners of the basement. That in itself is creepy and makes one wonder why the table was stored that way. Also at this reassembled table the dinner settings are continuously moved around for the morning workers to find. The silverware placement is traditional American style, but when the workers come in for the morning shift, the silverware is set in the old English style. Reminder: Captain John Joseph Willie Townshend was born and raised in England.

35

The self-closing Bible in the main dining room is said to be set at Captain Townshend's favorite verse. If the pages are turned, the book slams shut. The overly pungent smell of cigars hits visitors right in the face, even though no smoking is allowed in the building. Captain Townshend's wife, Ruth Montgomery DuVall, made sure her husband did not smoke. Is he getting the last laugh now?

Another haunting phenomenon is the over-saturated smell of a "grandma's perfume." The team does not credit this one to Captain Townshend but rather to the female spirits reported to reside at Seul Choix.

Perhaps the most famous story of the lighthouse is the face in the mirror. A mirror located in one of the upstairs bedrooms, the very vanity mirror believed to be in Captain Townshend's room when he died, is said to have a face appear right in front of tours and workers.

The list of hauntings and stories at Seul Choix goes on and on, but we need to move on to what the UPPRS actually experienced there, and there is a lot of that to tell.

As the team unpacked its gear in the back rooms that would be their headquarters for the night, part of the group went with Marilyn to get the tour and stories. Those members were set with video and audio recorders, which they had going the entire walkthrough, as well as still cameras, and other essential gadgets in a ghost hunter's toolbox. The members who were downstairs setting up the gear barely had time to get the equipment set up when the two-way radios went off.

"You guys need to get up here, now!" The voice on the other end was team member Jason Fegan, sounding excited.

"What's going on?" answered Tim Ellis.

"The face! Marilyn thinks the face is starting to appear. GET UP HERE!"

At that moment it was like a scene from the fiestas of San Fermin and the running of the bulls. Five grown men tried to be the first up the narrow winding stairs to get a glimpse of what they had only read about up to this moment. Could this really be happening? Not 10 minutes after their first steps into the legendary lighthouse, and things were already getting creepy!

Once squeezed into the small upstairs bedroom, everyone's stare was fixed on the vanity mirror. In the mirror's upper righthand corner, there seemed to be a mist, or film, and within that, what appeared to be a face! Was a face really staring back at the team or was this merely a case of matrixing? Matrixing is also known as the Man in the Moon theory, in which the brain wants to make sense of what is seen by the eyes. The mind will not stop until it makes sense of something. It will look for recognizable shapes. Often, in the paranormal field, "faces" are seen in windows, or in mist and fog. Is this what was happening to the group? Or was the famous face making an appearance to welcome them?

As this strange event was happening in the mirror, one of the team members snapped a picture, capturing what everyone was seeing. As soon as that picture was taken, the new batteries in the camera went dead. Completely drained. That very moment, the new battery in the video camera was also drained to zero percent. Something removed the energy from those batteries. As this was going on, a member of the Gulliver Historical Society and a known medium in the area told the team that there was someone, or something, standing right behind him, over his right shoulder. Team members quickly took ambient and surface temperature readings of the area near the medium. The temperature proved to be 10 degrees colder than the rest of the room. Whether or not a face actually formed in the mirror, one thing was for sure, something strange was happening in that room, and the UPPRS had just received one hell of a welcome to Seul Choix Point Lighthouse.

Once things calmed down, and the team returned to setting up their equipment, they had to be wondering how the rest of the night could live up to what they had just experienced. Little did they know the events of the night were just beginning.

The night was still young while Tim Ellis and Steve LaPlaunt did some field work.

"Dude...Dude! Look!" said Steve, as he elbowed Tim.

As Tim turned and looked, there in front of them was a latched cabinet door slowly opening on its own. As the two watched in amazement, the air quickly filled with the smell of cigar smoke. The two longtime friends looked at each other with the biggest smile, knowing the captain was with them.

As the night rolled on, it was an evening of ebbs and flows of energy, as is often the case during a night of investigating. Weird events seem to happen in clusters. You can feel the energy increase, and experiences happen for the investigators. Then, as fast as it started, you will feel the energy leave like the air out of a balloon, and once again, everything goes quiet. The first night for the UPPRS at Seul Choix followed this exact formula.

Around 4:00 AM the team wanted to give one last big push before packing up the gear and heading home. They all met in the main living area for an EVP session.

"Son of a bitch," yelled Steve LaPlaunt, as he jumped out of his chair. "Something just grabbed my hand."

If any of the team felt tired or wanted to fall asleep at this point, that was all quickly erased. Before anyone could ask Steve what was wrong, or what happened, laughter replaced his fear. Embarrassment followed as he realized the ghostly hand that he thought reached out and touched his hand was nothing more than the digital camera lens closing on its own due to inactivity.

After a good laugh at Steve's expense, the team was quiet again, hoping for one final sign from the captain or any of the other resident ghosts. Around 4:30 AM the last sound the team needed to hear, to let them know it was time to get the hell out of there, happened. The noise first started out as a "low growl," stated Lance Brown, lead Tech Advisor. Everyone was at attention now. What was that sound? Where was it coming from? Then, another blast, and this time it was much louder.

"Dude...Brad! Wake up!" yelled Ted Ellis. "You're snoring, you idiot!"

"That's because it's time for bed, you idiot," mumbled Blair, grunting as he slowly pushed himself up off the antique couch.

The team quickly agreed. After all, the investigation was over 12 hours old, and the team was tired.

As any investigative team knows, the daunting task of turning on the lights and packing up the gear is not a favorite part of the night. Still, the team always prides itself on how quickly they can strike the gear and pack it up. This, of course, is much to the chagrin of head Techy Lance Brown, who also babysits and takes care of the hundreds and hundreds of dollars' worth of gear.

The last walk through to make sure all lights were off and doors locked was done by Tim Ellis. "I remember the feeling vividly," he said. "I was the last one out of the house, and I felt like I was the eight-year-old version of myself, running up the basement stairs in my childhood home, scared of the monsters that were behind me. As I walked through Seul Choix, I had an overwhelming feeling of not one, but multiple people behind me. I kept turning around, expecting to see people right there. The feeling built up inside me until I shut the front door and climbed in the van with the rest of the team. I have no doubt I was *not* alone as I shut the house down for the night."

It was 6:00 AM as the group started their drive home. Less than a mile down the long, dark, dirt road they were greeted by something lying in their way.

"What the hell is that?" Lance Brown, the volunteer driver, slowed and kept the headlights dead on it.

Bones! More specifically, a full ribcage that something had enjoyed right down to the bones!

"Wolves," one of the group yelled from the back of the van.

"YES!"

They all agreed that what they were staring at was the remnants of a deer, which was dinner for the wolves and dragged right into the middle of the road. Albeit a very natural thing in the U.P. of Michigan, it was still quite the ominous good-bye from the team's maiden voyage to Seul Choix Point Lighthouse!

It would be well over a year before the UPPRS would find their way back to the haunted lighthouse. During that time the team continued to grow in case counts and experience. Also during that time, the thought of getting back to Seul Choix never left their minds. It was almost as if the lighthouse was calling them back again—something the team believes still happens today.

The time finally came for the group to prepare for their return to Seul Choix, and this next trip holds the title of "Holy Sh$t, did you see that!" It was early summer. The team knew what to expect with the winding and narrowing dirt roads, but seeing the light tower appear over the trees was as exciting as the first time. "There she is," yelled Michelle Carrick, the team's lone female member, and just like the first time, the van went silent as everyone just stared at the giant looking down on them over the evergreen and maple trees.

Much like last time, the team was greeted with the smile and hugs of Marilyn Fischer, someone they had grown very fond of, and she of them. A real friendship had been made. With Marilyn this time was another new friend of the team, author Jan Langley. Jan and Marilyn visited with the group as they unpacked the gear and set it up for another long night. Once the team was set and ready for a night alone with Captain Townshend and his lighthouse, Marilyn and Jan said their goodbyes and the place was theirs. By plan, this time the team brought cheap cigars as a trigger to bring the captain out to play. Using a "trigger" is very common in paranormal investigating, where a group will use an object that the spirit enjoyed before their death. Knowing the captain enjoyed cigars, the team wanted to use that as their trigger.

Everyone left the living quarters and wanted to let their cameras and audio recorders run, with no one, well... no living person, in the lighthouse. The group walked to the north side parking lot, where they had parked the van. The conversation was heavy among them, as they prepared for the evening. They grabbed the cheap cigars and handed

40

them out. Keep in mind, no one on the team smokes, so this was a scene right out of an after-school special, where kids are smoking for the first time, and trying to look cool between their chokes and coughs.

"Captain Townshend," said Tim Ellis, "we want to thank you for allowing us to come back for another visit, and we hope you will want to come and visit with us as you did on our first visit. In your honor, we have brought cigars which we are going to smoke now, outside, like you had to do so many times."

The team lit the cigars, saluted the captain, and the conversation quickly resumed. The plan was to let the equipment do their stuff, alone in the lighthouse, for an hour, before they went back in, but that was going to be cut short, quickly!

On the north side of the lighthouse, where the team was located, four windows face the parking lot. The farthest one on the left is in the formal kitchen, where the family cooked and ate. The next two to the right are in the formal dining room, where the Bible sits that is reported to close on its own. The final window, the farthest to the right, is in the back kitchen where the help worked and ate. It was this window that was about to begin what to this day would be the most prominent paranormal moment for the team.

Tim Ellis and Matt Barr were both looking at the far right window at the moment a dark figure inside the house walked by, heading toward the formal dining room.

"Did you see that?" Tim asked Matt.

"You mean the figure that just walked right in front of us, *inside the house?* Yeah...I saw it!"

By then, the rest of the team realized something had just happened and were filled in immediately. Knowing that no living person was in that house at that moment, the entire team sat gazing at the next set of windows, in the formal dining room, which had the curtains closed. As seven pairs of eyes stared at those windows, the curtains were pulled back by an unseen entity and stayed open for what seemed an eternity to

41

the team as they sat, stunned, all watching the same thing. Someone, or something, was in that house and had opened the curtains to gaze upon the stunned team. The curtain slowly went back into position, and the team stayed silent for a brief moment. Then, like children on Christmas morning, they began to yell, asking each other, "Did you just see that? Did we all just see that?" The answer was a resounding, YES! After a moment of excitement and expletives being shared among the team, it quickly hit them—they had to get in that lighthouse, stat!

Tim Ellis and Steve LaPlaunt were the first to the front door. They went in while the rest of the group stayed outside and surrounded the house to make sure no one sneaked out, in case someone was trying to pull a fast one on them.

"We are always asked if we have ever been so scared on an investigation that we wanted to quit doing what we do," said Tim. "The short answer is, NO. But, this particular moment at Seul Choix is probably as close to that moment as we have come. I remember reaching for the doorknob, about to go in with Steve, and not knowing what we would see as soon as that door was open. I remember looking at Steve and asking, "Dude....why do we do this to ourselves? Two very nervous and excited laughs followed as I turned the doorknob."

The adrenaline was at its highest point for the guys as they slowly opened the front door. Entering like a cop would at a crime scene, the two moved in, and it hit them immediately! It wasn't something they saw, but rather something they smelled: the over-pungent smell of lilac. But not the amazing smell that comes from the God-given lilac bush, but rather the cheap, overly floral smell of the perfume that all grandmothers end up wearing at some point.

"It was as if someone's grandmother walked right past us the moment we opened the door," said Steve. "It played right into all the accounts of people smelling that perfume throughout the lighthouse when no one else was around."

Further investigation of the house found no other person inside, and sadly, the post-investigation review of all the video also showed no one in the lighthouse at the time of the incident. However, every member of the UPPRS will tell you exactly what they all witnessed that night!

It would be another summer, winter, and spring before the team found themselves back on the road to Seul Choix. However, this time, the investigation would be a little bit different. They were accompanied by the sister-author team of Kathleen Tedson and Bev Rydel. They were working on their follow-up book for *Haunted Travels of Michigan,* a wonderful book based on investigations they went on with other teams throughout the state. The book uses an interactive concept in which the reader is given specific codes to punch into the accompanying website to view suspect photos and video and to listen to possible EVPs caught on audio. The book was such a favorite among the readers that they were now working on *Haunted Travels of Michigan, Volume II,* and this particular investigation with the UPPRS may be found in those pages.

Once again the team was greeted by Marilyn with smiles and hugs, and the unloading of the equipment began. In comparison to other visits, this particular night started out relatively quiet for the team. Around 1:00 AM the entire team, along with the two authors, Bev and Kat, were gathered around headquarters, allowing their recording equipment to do their jobs. Everyone was chatting and laughing when the faint sound of music was first heard by Tim.

"It was very light," he said, "like the sound a music box would make. I seriously thought I was hearing things, then all of a sudden I heard the words I hoped to hear from someone else."

"Are you guys hearing music?" asked Matt McLeod.

The room went completely quiet, and there it was, for everyone to hear, a faint instrumental song that would come from an antique music box. The group quickly split up. Two headed upstairs, two stayed on the main floor, two ran to the basement, and the rest ran outside to check the grounds. Within minutes the music was gone, and despite the group's best efforts, the source was never found. Just as on the previous trip, another unexplained event was witnessed by the entire group, and once again, no natural cause could be seen. The mystery of Seul Choix once again came out and said hello to the team!

There is one theory about this phantom noise that team president Tim Ellis puts some faith in. He said, "Months before the investigation, I had tasked our Tech Team with a particular project." (The UPPRS Tech Team consists of Head Tech Manager Lance Brown and two fellow nerds, Jason Fegan, and Matt Barr.) "I have always said," Tim continued, "that I would put these three up against anyone in the field. With any task asked of them, they put on their super nerd hats and never cease to impress us. This particular task was one that at that time had never been tried before. There were no blueprints to go from.

"I asked them to create for us a portable energy field. Something that we could move from room to room to produce high energy spots, in the hope that spirits could use that energy to manifest or communicate. The idea of high EMF fields possibly being used by ghosts to manifest and communicate has long been a theory in the field. And keep in mind, this was long before the days of the EM pump, and other mass-produced EMF field generators were created and on the market to purchase for $19.99.

"Within twenty-four hours the tech team was already sending us sketches and ideas on how to make this happen. Within a week, they had our prototype created and ready to come to Seul Choix. I remember Lance telling me that no one but himself was to operate the 'Beast' they had created. I believe he told me it could melt a small village if not used properly. As I laughed and worried at the same time, I assured him it was all his to use.

"That particular night at the lighthouse we had the UPPRS version of a mobile EMF hooked up in the basement with a camera pointed right at it. Although it never gave us anything substantial on the camera, I do believe it very well could have been the energy needed to help bring that music to us that night."

The seasons would come and go two more times before the team would head back to their favorite place. This trip would be the smallest team they had brought. Just four members made the trip: Ryan McLeod, Brad Blair, Steve LaPlaunt and Tim Ellis. The idea this time was to always keep a team of two in the house and a team of two outside on the grounds. As usual, Steve and Tim were paired off, and Brad and Ryan would work together as the other team.

The night had its usual possible footsteps and phantom smells, but the moment that stands out from this investigation includes a very prominent light pole in the front yard. It's a large light that can flood most of the front yard and is on a timer to come on at dusk. The central control of the light is in the lighthouse and can be prevented from turning on automatically. That was done early in the arrival of the team, knowing they would be doing work in the yard.

Tim and Steve were outside doing some EVP work when they asked the foremost question asked by any investigative team, "Can you please give us a sign that you are with us?" At that moment, the front yard was illuminated from the light pole just to their side. As usual with this team, after a few expletives were shared between Steve and Tim, Steve quickly radioed up to Brad and Ryan to ask if they had just turned on the main switch to light outside. Brad quickly radioed back, saying, *no*, they were doing an EVP session, and Steve should go kick rocks (it wasn't that friendly of a comment) for interrupting it. Steve then asked Brad what the particular question was that he had just asked. Brad answered, "If you are here with us, can you make the light outside turn on!"

Once again, the two friends just stared at each other with a smile, knowing exactly what was going on. It was Captain Townshend and the other spirits of Seul Choix Point Lighthouse saying hello to their old friends from the Upper Peninsula Paranormal Research Society. The team has never gone there and not come back without some kind of unexplained event or events that always keeps them wanting to go back for more. The team has dubbed Seul Choix Point Lighthouse their very own Disneyland.

Perhaps the creepiest picture from Seul Choix in the group's possession was not even one of their own photos. It was shared with Marilyn Fischer by a visitor to the lighthouse, who was taking pictures of the light tower from the front yard. In one of her photos she noticed what looked like a figure standing at the very top, looking down through the windows. She gave the picture to Marilyn, who quickly contacted the UPPRS. Once that photo was blown up it appeared to show a figure at the top of the lighthouse looking down—but not a human-looking figure.

The stories and legends of Seul Choix Point Lighthouse were countless before the UPPRS ever set foot there. Since that first visit until today, the group continues to add to these fantastic events at this beautiful, historical, and very active location. As of the writing of this book, the team is preparing for yet another return visit to their Disneyland. Do yourself a favor. Program Seul Choix Point Lighthouse on your GPS and make the trip. While you are there, be vigilant and watch for the signs, and be sure to tell Captain Townshend that his friends from the UPPRS say hello and that they will be visiting him very soon.

If you would like more information on the shared haunted tales of Seul Choix, there are some fun reads and DVDs to watch, such as a book penned by the president of the Gulliver Historical Society, Marilyn Fischer, *Spirits at Seul Choix Pointe: True Lighthouse Stories*, which contains firsthand accounts and visitors' stories shared with her. *True Lighthouse Hauntings* is a DVD filmed and directed by Don Hermanson of Keweenaw Video Productions. Captain Joseph Willie Townshend is so popular that even a children's book was written called *The Captain and Harry: a Trembling Tail of Thieves*, written by Jan Langley, which tells the tale of a young mouse who lives in the lighthouse and befriends the ghost of Captain Townshend.

MISSION POINT RESORT, MACKINAC ISLAND

For centuries prior to the first Europeans stepping foot on the North American continent, the Ojibwa people traversed the waterways now known as the Great Lakes to visit the sacred island of Mi-She-Mi-Ki-Nock, The Great Turtle. This was a sacred land, home to the Gitche Manitou and the burial ground for tribal chiefs and their families. Many generations were brought to the island for noble burial ceremonies before the strange faces of French voyageurs and missionaries began appearing, changing life forever. What was once a place of solace became a trading depot and eventually a military outpost, building over the unmarked graves of those long passed, stirring their restless spirits to roam the land of the living once again.

Mackinac Island sits at the top of Lake Huron, just east of the Straits of Mackinac where lakes Michigan and Huron meet, and the Mackinac Bridge, the longest suspension bridge in the western hemisphere, connects Michigan's two peninsulas. Today, better than

80 percent of the nearly four square miles that compose the island are owned by the Mackinac Island State Park Commission, and the entire island is listed as a National Historic Landmark.

Mackinac Island. Credit: Don Hermanson Keweenaw Video Productions.

Accessible only by boat or small plane (or by snowmobile in the winter, once the straits freeze over), the island has enforced a ban on motor vehicles since 1898. Transportation on Mackinac consists of horse drawn carriages and bicycles, adding to the Victorian charm which has made it not only the top tourist destination in Michigan, but also recently saw it named the Top Summer Destination in America by TripAdvisor, as well as Best Island in the U.S. by Conde Nast Traveler, and one of the most tourist-friendly locations in the country by Expedia.

The ferry services run ships seemingly non-stop during the warm summer months, carrying thousands of tourists every day from

Mackinaw City in the Lower Peninsula and St. Ignace in the U.P. to enjoy all the outdoor activities and charm the island has become famous for. The packed streets and full hotels are typical of summers on Mackinac, quite the contrast to the island's early days and its original visitors.

No one knows for sure when the native people began venturing to Mackinac Island. Their legends regard it as a spiritual place, the residence of the Gitche Manitou. Because this was home to the Great Spirit, it was believed that the dead who were buried there were watched over in their eternal rest by the Manitou himself. Tribespeople would present offerings there to the Great Spirit in exchange for his aid in guaranteeing bountiful harvests of fish and wild game through the coming season.

The Gitche Manitou was not the sole supernatural resident of the island, however. A feared race of giants was believed to inhabit the cliffs and large rock formations of Mackinac, and Puk-wudj-in-i-nees, the Vanishing Little People, were said to roam its inland forest. Although tales of these giants waned long ago, there is still a belief that the Pukwudjis continue to inhabit the island. Now more often referred to as fairies, these wandering lights are reported by residents and tourists alike, leading the curious into the woods or off along the lakeshore. With such beings thought to inhabit the island, generation after generation of native peoples have held Mackinac in high regard as a place of great spiritual energy.

It was the early 1600s when strangers began to emerge from the waterways. French explorers seeking new trade routes had discovered the Great Lakes and their tribal communities. These explorers would return home with tales of the massive inland seas of fresh water, all teeming with fish, the surrounding forests abundant with wild game and fertile soil, prompting the influx of Europeans to the Great Lakes basin.

The voyageurs, fur traders of predominately French origin, first recorded stopping off on Mackinac Island in 1634. From their perspective, it was an ideal location to establish a trading post. Not only did the waters of lakes Huron and Michigan join here, but also a short trek north brought them to St. Mary's River, which connected Lake Superior to the lower lakes. They were the first Europeans to set up camp on the island, and the first to experience its mysteries.

Early traders were warned by natives to beware of the Paw-gwa-tchaw-nish-naw-boy, wild supernatural beings which roamed the island. The Frenchmen dismissed the tale as a fabrication, just a story invented by the tribes to persuade non-natives to avoid their sacred land, but tales passed on by the raconteurs of these early trade groups suggest there may have been more to the warning than mere superstition or legend.

Tales passed from one trade group to another of the numerous encounters early voyageurs had with what they called "Les Dames Blanches," the White Ladies, small white lights flittering about the woods, seemingly trying to lead the men off the trails and into the depths of the forest. More than one explorer found themselves lost in the woods at night after pursuing these luminescent forms. Natives, upon hearing these tales, recognized these to be encounters with the Puck-wudj-in-i-nees, and warned that interactions with them not be taken lightly.

A much more frightening tale of early Mackinac involved a young voyageur named Jacque, who was venturing between two camps on his way to settle into his tent after a long night of song and story around a roaring campfire. As he made his way down a forest trail, something stirred on the wooded hill above. Quickening his pace, he heard the sound of breaking branches following close behind. Thinking a member of his crew was playing a trick on him, his courage returned and he came to a sudden halt. Turning to confront his stalker, Jacque was greeted by a deep throaty growl and the sight of two yellow eyes just above him on the hillside! His heart raced as he was set upon by a large, hairy creature, a beast which appeared to be the largest wolf the voyageur had ever seen! Massive fangs gleamed in the moonlight as dagger-like claws ripped through his side and face! Acting on pure instinct, Jacque pulled his knife from the sheath in his belt and slashed wildly toward the creature. As the blade made contact, the beast let out a hair-raising howl and fled back into the brush. It was then that Jacque came to the startling realization that the creature he had thought to be a large wolf was running on two legs!

Wounded and in a state of shock, Jacque stumbled back to the campfire, seeking help from his comrades. After cleaning and bandaging the wounds, deeming them mostly superficial, and treating the pain with a few pulls from a brown jug, Jacque related the story of his encounter to his fellow traders. When he came to the ending, he hesitated. Although fearing his comrades would deem him mad, he continued on. "When I slashed the beast with my knife, it howled in pain and ran off…on two legs!" As the men stared at Jacque, the oldest of the crew gasped out two words: "Loup Garou!" The attention now turned to the eldest voyageur, as he continued with an explanation. "You were attacked by a Loup Garou; half man, half wolf. The Indians 'round these parts call them Bearwalkers. Say they can change from man to beast at will. Nasty creatures that you'd do best to avoid."

These stories and more were passed down by the voyageurs and became island legend, but how much is fact versus fiction in these tales? The White Ladies can easily be related to the Puckwudjis, simply the European version of an established native entity. And the Loup Garou, the French equivalent of a werewolf, is viewed as the bearwalker of the regional tribes.

As more European settlers and traders made their way to the Great Lakes, Mackinac Island developed into a key destination. For the voyageurs, it became a place for extended stops where they were now able to conduct negotiations, restock supplies, and plan their next journey. It was a central point to the water routes connecting three of the Great Lakes.

The strategic significance of the location was not lost to the British, either. Desiring a military outpost to protect their trade routes from Canada into the Great Lakes, the British Army established a fort on the island in 1780. They held this post until 1796, when American forces ousted them and gained control. The Americans would hold the fort for 16 years until the first U.S. land engagement of the War of 1812 saw British forces retake Fort Mackinac and hold it for the remainder of the war. After that it was returned to the Americans, and the British troops were relocated to nearby Drummond Island. American forces continued to operate the fort as an active military outpost until 1895.

51

Through military squabbles and changes of control, Mackinac remained a center for commerce amongst fur traders, natives, and upstart businessmen attempting to conduct commerce with both. It also became a regular stop for Christian missionaries who were being sent into rural areas with the goal of converting the Native Americans to Christianity.

When Reverend William Montague Ferry was assigned to Mackinac in 1823, it was with a two-fold mission: not just to convert the natives, but to educate them as well. The reverend acquired a piece of land on the southeast corner of the island and set to work constructing his schoolhouse. William and his wife, Amanda, would oversee construction of the combined school and boarding house, and in 1825 Mission House School was opened to the children of the island and surrounding territories with an inaugural class of 112 native students.

The Ferrys were dedicated to their faith, establishing the first protestant church on the island and overseeing a congregation that at one point ministered to nearly 100 parishioners as well as the school children. The Mission Church, built in the New England Colonial style, still stands near the entrance to Mission Point, and is listed in the National Register of Historic Places.

In the 1830s, the island faced a period of significant change. The fur trade had undergone a steep decline, and the major investors who had established agencies and developed the local community were now closing their doors and recalling their agents. The overall population was on the decline, along with the need for the church and boarding school.

William and Amanda were faced with the reality that a dedicated school on the island was no longer feasible. In 1834 they left the island for good. The Mission House School was shut down three years later and would sit empty for the following decade.

As the business model exploited by the original settlers faded away, new employment opportunities emerged in the Midwest. Major cities including Detroit and Chicago were embracing the industrial age, and those seeking work flocked to these areas by the thousands. New innovations produced new wealth, and the emerging upper and middle classes of the mid-1800s sought out places of leisure. With easy access via steamship from burgeoning metropolitan areas, Mackinac Island became just such a place.

Visitors seeking relaxation in the clean fresh air and quiet atmosphere of the north found Mackinac a desirable place to spend summer months away from the crowded streets, polluted air, and everyday hustle and bustle of big city life. This new wave of tourism brought a rebirth to Mackinac, along with which came the demand for more lodging establishments. The abandoned Mission House was about to get a second chance at life.

It was 1847 when businessman Edward Frank purchased the Mission House property and set about renovating the former school into a hotel, refurbishing the original structure and adding on entirely new wings. The finished product was known as Mission Hotel, which offered travelers the modern conveniences of the day along with a breathtaking view of Lake Huron. The Mission House entertained tourists under the ownership of the Frank family for nearly a century, right up until the days of the Great Depression. With the nation in the depths of a financial crisis, vacation was no longer an option for most people, and the tourism business on the island was hit hard by the lack of visitors. The heirs of Edward Frank were forced to close Mission Hotel, and once again the property sat empty.

The next transformation of the Mission Point property came in 1954, when, after sitting empty for a number of years, it was purchased by an organization that would make major changes to the area, constructing many of the buildings which make up the current resort.

The Moral Re-Armament (MRA), a cult-like evangelical organization, made the decision to relocate their world headquarters to Mission Point, an area well known to the leadership of the MRA which had been holding retreats on the island since the mid-1940s.

The group quickly settled into the former Mission Hotel and hired contractors to begin making their grand view of MRA

53

headquarters a reality. First, an 800-seat theater was constructed in order to hold events, including propaganda plays and films which were mostly composed by high ranking members. The following year, construction began on the main lodge. This impressive structure, the centerpiece of which now houses the grand lobby and guest registration for the resort, was built to resemble a massive Native American teepee. The MRA used this structure as a marketing tool for their new base of operations, claiming that they were fulfilling the Indian prophecy that "Someday, on the east end of the island, a great teepee will be erected. All nations will come there and learn about peace."

The group continued to expand the point, adding another lodge, several outbuildings, and a film studio where MRA plays could be produced into motion pictures. They would host dignitaries from around the world at their new, state-of-the-art headquarters, making every effort to spread their views and win support of the wealthy and influential.

As a cultural change swept America in the 1960s, the influence of the MRA and similar groups began to wane. The younger generation rejected the views of their parents and embraced new beliefs. With their flock dwindling, the MRA departed Mission Point and relocated their headquarters to Switzerland, severing all ties with the island.

Over the following decade, the former campus of the MRA would see several incarnations. In 1966 the property would become Mackinac College, a liberal arts school that would graduate only one class, closing its doors in 1970 due to lack of funding. In 1972, a televangelist purchased the property to be used as a bible college, which was also short lived.

By the mid-1970s, the number of tourists visiting the island was hitting record numbers. An investment firm purchased the then-vacant property and with renovations, reopened it to the public as the Mackinac Hotel and Conference Center, which, under new ownership again in 1987, was re-named Mission Point Resort. The resort now occupies every structure on the property with the exception of the 1825 Mission House, which was deeded to the Mackinac Island State Park Commission and is used to house seasonal staff.

Mission Point Resort today. Credit: Don Hermanson Keweenaw Video Productions.

Today, Mission Point Resort is one of the premiere lodging establishments on Mackinac Island, boasting five restaurants, a spa, health club, and even an 18-hole waterfront mini-golf course. It has received the prestigious honor of being named "Best Place to Stay in Michigan" by Conde Nast Traveler, a location enjoyed by visitors from around the world, and possibly beyond?

It is hard to pinpoint when ghostly activity was first reported at the point. Apparitions sighted today are so varied in appearance and dress, it's difficult imagining the hauntings not being from multiple time periods.

One of the regulars among Mission Point ghost sightings is the spirit of an older gentleman referred to as The Judge, most often reported in the main lodge. According to Mission Point Conference Service Manager, Pat Driscoll, "A number of people have said they've seen a gentleman walking around in a long black robe, like a judge's robe, so that's what they call him now, The Judge." Given the history of the property, could this be a missionary from the early days of the school? Long dark robes were common attire amongst them.

*Aerial view of Mission Point Resort. Credit: Don Hermanson
Keweenaw Video Productions.*

The ghost of a young girl seemingly makes the theater her home. Captured in both pictures and audio over the years by visiting paranormal enthusiasts, she is something of a mystery. Her dress appears to be from the Victorian era, and although often playful, she is reported to give the sense that she is searching for someone or something and is more likely to interact with women than men.

The most prevalent apparition reported at the point is thought to be tied to a tragedy from the days of Mackinac College. In 1967, a student named Craig went missing from the campus, and was later found dead on the bluff above from an apparently self-inflicted gunshot wound. As the story goes, Craig had fallen in love with another student who had no romantic desire toward him. Heartbroken from her rejection and unable to persuade the young lady to reconsider her feelings, he fell into a deep depression. Although there has been speculation over the years that foul play may have been involved, the case was ruled a suicide and remains closed.

Since Craig's death, sightings of a young man have been reported throughout the resort. One of the chefs who was unknowingly housed in Craig's old dorm room reported strange activity on a regular basis, including the vision of a translucent figure walking across the room and through a wall. What was thought to be the apparition of a young man appeared one day in a women's steam room, then quickly disappeared. Whether these encounters are connected to Craig or not, most male apparitions spotted on the resort grounds are automatically associated with him.

The UPPRS was thrilled at the opportunity to investigate the resort: not only would they be working after the resort had closed for the season, giving them full run of the campus, but filmmaker Don Hermanson was once again joining the team to record the investigation for a project he'd been filming on Mackinac Island hauntings.

As late fall arrived and plans were made for what was to be their largest investigation to date, Tim received an unwelcome phone call. "Hey, this is Laurie with Mission Point. Hate to be the bearer of bad news, but we've been contacted by a production company that wants to film an episode at the resort for some show called *Ghost Hunters*. They'll be here the week you planned on coming, and we're locking everything down for the winter as soon as they leave." The much anticipated investigation would now have to wait until spring.

Winter came and went, and when the first passenger ferry set out for the island in April, the Yoopers were on it. With no automobiles on the island, arrangements had been made for horse drawn carriages to transport the team and their equipment from the dock to Mission Point. None of the storefronts and few lodging establishments were open for the season, giving Mackinac Island the atmosphere of a ghost town; empty streets and boarded up windows greeted them as the horses clomped along the silent road, a steady rain falling on the Yoopers team and their exposed equipment totes.

As the carriages approached the resort, the immensity of the job awaiting them became intimidatingly clear: a multitude of large buildings, all with ghostly tales, needed to be covered in the short time they were allotted. Although the resort had been kind enough to arrange two large suites for the team to stay in, it was obvious there wouldn't be much time for sleep.

A small but central room in the theater building would be team headquarters for the night. Equipment was unloaded and setup underway as Brad and Tim, along with Don, who had already begun filming, were given a tour of the property by the one supervisor who had already returned to the island to prepare for the upcoming flood of tourists. Once the trio returned to base and briefed the group on the layout and "hot spots" of each building, a plan of action was laid out and the UPPRS broke off into groups to begin their investigation.

Tim headed out into the rain, making his way to the main lodge along with Lance and Matty McLeod, the team's new rookie investigator who was along for his first major investigation. The massive lobby, normally welcoming with its two fireplaces providing warmth and ambiance, stood cold and dark, the heating system not yet reactivated for the season. "Let's hit the kitchen first, and work our way down through the lower levels," Tim directed, remembering the stories kitchen staff had shared about items being moved and disembodied voices startling the staff in that area.

The guys proceeded from the lobby and through the empty dining room to the kitchen entrance, the door to which was propped open with a large, heavy stone. As Matty entered the kitchen, a loud scraping sound broke the silence. Behind him, the door slid shut, taking the heavy stone along the floor with it. Tim and Lance, still on the outside, had witnessed the moving door and now stood puzzled.

"What just happened?" Lance inquired.

Matty reemerged from the kitchen, wondering the same thing. "I didn't touch anything!" he stated defensively.

"No, we have it on camera," Lance said. "There's no way that door could have moved on its own."

After resetting the stone door block, the team made several attempts to recreate a scenario where the door would slide shut without being pushed. Each attempt failed. After making note of the time and occurrence, the trio continued on into the bowels of the lodge.

Meanwhile, back at the theater Brad, Steve, and Ryan had made their way to the balcony in the main auditorium. Taking into account the reports of a young girl being spotted there, Brad had brought along a doll to set up as a trigger object, which he hoped would entice the girl to communicate. "We brought this for you. We call her Mini-Michelle. We just hope you'll take a few minutes to talk with us," Brad said to the empty space in front of him.

Steve LaPlaunt investigating the balcony in the Mission Point Theater.
Don Hermanson Keweenaw Video Productions.

Taking seats in the middle row, the guys began an EVP session in hopes of learning who the girl was, and why she was drawn to the theater. Steve, breaking the one-way conversation, stood up and rubbed his arms. "Is it getting colder in here?" he asked, shivering.

"It's dropped a full three degrees in the last minute or so," Ryan confirmed, glancing at the ambient thermometer in his hand.

Hearing a loud sigh from behind them, the group turned to face the back of the balcony. There, in the top row of seating, a dark shadow began moving down the aisle and disappeared into the wall.

"Did you guys see that?" Brad shouted, already knowing by their expressions that everyone present had indeed witnessed the figure.

Quickly returning to the EVP session, questions were directed toward whatever was the entity they had just witnessed. Unfortunately, when the recordings were played back, the excited voices of the three investigators were the only sounds the recorder had picked up.

As the temperature rebounded to where it had been prior to the encounter, the group grabbed what equipment they'd brought, leaving the doll perched on the balcony railing in plain view of a surveillance camera, and moved on to their next location, adrenaline still pumping from their first experience of what was to be a long, memorable night.

After regrouping for a quick team debriefing and some much needed coffee (the rain had now turned to a heavy, wet snow), the groups moved out to their next locations. With an investigation of this scale, no member could be spared to observe the monitors for the night. That footage would need to be reviewed after the weekend had wrapped up.

The Straits Lodge, boasting 133 guest rooms and suites, was to be investigated by Jason, Matt, and Michelle. Even with most of the hotel rooms inaccessible, it was sure to be a daunting task to cover the multiple floors of winding halls and public areas. Bundled up against the cold and loaded down with equipment, the threesome headed out.

Exiting the theater building on their way to the lodge, they were about to confront their first "activity" of the night as a stack of boxes just outside the door was heaved over right in front of the trio, sending the guys back against the wall and Michelle airborne as she leapt into the still open entryway! This event was immediately followed by another box flying off the next pile, as a loud commotion ensued. The team glared transfixed at what seemed to be an animated pile of cardboard containers determined to scare them off. As the last stack wobbled, the "ghost" emerged; a giant raccoon, the size of a small car, according to Matt, ran out from under the trash pile and off into the adjacent trees, leaving the startled trio to regain their composure.

With the mystery of the haunted boxes solved, they returned focus to the task at hand: Straits Lodge. The plan was to begin with the top floor where the specter of a young man was most often reported and work their way down floor by floor.

"This place reminds me of *The Shining*," Michelle observed, noting the similarities to the classic Stanley Kubrick film as they ventured through the top level. "A big empty hotel in a deserted area. I keep expecting the elevator doors to open and those creepy twins to walk out!"

Creepy atmosphere aside, it was an uneventful start to their trek through the lodge until the three investigators descended to the second floor's main stairwell, where a faint sound caught their attention. "Did you guys hear something?" Jason inquired as the group froze in place.

"Yah, it sounded like two people talking," Matt replied. "Play back your recorder and see if we caught it."

Jason reviewed the audio, which revealed a faint male voice captured under the trio's conversation. They attempted an EVP session, but were once again greeted by silence.

Energized from the brief encounter, they continued to work their way through the second then first floors. Once again, all was quiet until they approached the stairs.

"I'm hearing it again," Michelle mumbled under her breath.

This time, there was no mistaking the muffled sound of a conversation, followed by the distinct voice of...Bob Marley? As the group entered the basement, they were greeted by two men in the hallway, room doors wide open, drinks in hand, and music blaring. After brief introductions, it was learned that several of the resort employees had returned early to begin preparations for the season. Unbeknownst to the UPPRS team, these staff members were being housed in the basement quarters beneath Straits Lodge.

"Afraid this will discredit any other audio footage we picked up, outside of a direct answer to our EVP questioning," Jason stated, pointing out that any other voices may well have emanated from the workers rather than the dearly departed.

"That's strike two for the night." Matt joked as they headed back up to the lobby. "Should we head back to headquarters before we go down swinging?"

"Might as well," replied Jason.

They exited back into the snow with no paranormal evidence, but with two encounters that were sure to get a laugh from the rest of the team.

Back in the theater building, Brad, Steve, and Ryan, this time accompanied by Don and his camera, were investigating smaller rooms that bordered the auditorium. They were also running dry of any paranormal activity.

Finishing their rounds in a room to the rear of the auditorium, which was being used to store old film equipment and furnishings, Brad made one final plea to any unseen entities among them. "We're heading back to base now. If you're with us, please let us know."

Seemingly in answer, a lamp in the back corner of the room lit up briefly then went dark. Don honed his camera on the lamp as Brad began questioning the light fixture. "Was that intentional?"

Again, the lamp went on and off. Ryan switched on the audio recorder as Steve observed his EMF meter, watching for any change in the room's energy levels.

"Are you a female?" Brad inquired.

The lamp remained dark.

"Male?" he continued.

The light came back to life.

"Were you a resident of the island?"

No reply.

"Were you a part of the MRA organization?"

Again, there was no reply. The questioning continued until it was apparent that whoever had manipulated the light was no longer interested, or possibly able, to continue communicating.

"That was...interesting," said Ryan as they left the room, heading back toward base.

"Ya," replied Don, "and I caught the whole thing on camera. Going to be great for the documentary!"

Night had turned into early morning, and it was time to meet up with the others to plan the final stage of the investigation. Entering the room which housed their headquarters, the foursome was greeted by Tim, Lance, and Matty, who were finishing off what remained of the team's refreshments. After returning from Straits Lodge earlier than anticipated, Jason, Matt, and Michelle had already ventured back out to the auditorium where the team planned to regroup for one final session. More than 12 hours had passed since the start of the investigation, with several uneventful rounds mixed in with the active outings, and not even the gallons of coffee consumed could keep the ghost hunters vertical much longer. It was time to wrap things up.

Upon entering the auditorium, the guys were given a "hush" signal from Matt, pointing out Michelle was into an EVP session on the stage. Motioning the team back out the side door, Matt explained that when his group had entered the auditorium, they witnessed a shadow figure move through one of the rows and found several of the seats pushed down. When they began the initial EVP session, the answers they received were from a muffled feminine voice, and all replies were coming from questions asked by Michelle, so she was now conducting a solo session.

The group reentered the room as Michelle finished up her questioning. Playing back the audio revealed more of the same: a female voice which seemingly responded to her but was too soft and garbled to make out many of the words.

As the combined UPPRS spread out for one final sweep of the theater, soft footsteps were heard from the balcony. Ryan, who was standing near the stage, turned and began repeatedly snapping still pictures in that direction, as Matt and Matty made their way up the staircase to confirm they were not hearing an animal or other unwanted visitor. They weren't. The balcony was empty with nothing out of place except one seat in the front row which had been pushed down since the team members had last been there.

Another EVP session was conducted with no luck. It was finally time to tear down the equipment, pack the totes, and catch a couple hours of sleep before the carriage arrived to haul the team down the now snow-covered roads to the ferry dock.

The weary group made their way to the Straits Lodge where two rooms had been provided for the team. Upon entering their wing of the building, Brad noticed that the door to room 2200 was ajar. This suite had been noted as one of the areas where paranormal activity was often reported. In the episode of *Ghost Hunters* filmed at the resort, one of the cast members stayed in 2200 and caught video footage of a light turning on and off by itself throughout the night. Slipping away from the others, Brad entered the room and found although there was little heat, it was already made up for the season. Perfect! "Not only was this one of the most haunted rooms on the property, but if nobody noticed, I'd be able to spend a few hours in it alone." Brad recalls. Throwing his jacket on a chair and sliding into bed, he was just about to turn out the light when the door flew open and Tim and Matty stormed in.

"Nice try!" Tim said with a laugh. "Everyone else is crammed into those other rooms. Nobody's sleeping alone tonight." Tim crawled into the bed as Matty curled up on the cold leather loveseat.

After a couple uneventful hours of shut-eye (even if a poltergeist had banged on the walls, the exhausted guys would likely have slept through it), the blaring of the alarm signaled it was time to prepare for the trip back to the boat.

Matty, shivering on his makeshift bed, wrapped in the light blanket he'd found in a closet, was the first to rise. "Man, I didn't sleep at all! It's freezing in here!"

"I didn't think it was too bad," Brad replied, crawling out from under the heavy comforter.

"Look at that," Tim added, pointing to a heavy woolen blanket on the bed. "Must have been sleeping on top of that all night. Guess you could have used it, rookie."

Matty looked on, too exhausted to be angry. "I just want to get home to my own bed and sleep for a week!"

When the carriage reached the ferry dock, the team was greeted by a deckhand with the unwelcome news that due to the high winds, it would be a rough five-mile trip back to the mainland. The team hunkered down in the lower section of the ferry and braced for the bumpy ride back.

As waves washed over the windows and the boat teetered back and forth, Don decided he needed to capture this voyage on video. After filming the team, he made his way toward the rear deck.

"Do you really think that's a good idea?" asked Matt, whose complexion was already a light green from fighting off seasickness.

"I just need to catch some footage of the waves with the island in the background," Don replied as he headed out the rear door.

The team watched; observing Don through the porthole window. At first, he was seen holding the commercial-grade camera on his shoulder, then suddenly he disappeared! Fearing he went overboard, Lance rushed to the door and found him lying on the deck, having fallen when the last huge wave rocked the ship.

"Almost lost my camera!" Don yelled, holding up his prized piece of equipment.

"We almost lost you!" Lance returned, helping him through the hatch and back to his seat where he'd wait out the rest of the journey, sore and wet from his impact with the steel floor.

After a few days of rest, the collected audio and video of the excursion was split up to be reviewed. Often, there is little captured on either which was not experienced during the investigation; however, that was not the case with Mission Point.

The audio had been downloaded to a computer, and although it was able to be "cleaned up," the voices which had been captured were still indiscernible. The video was another matter entirely. After several hours of stillness, one camera, which had been positioned in a hall in the lower level of the main lodge, moved. Although nobody was present, the camera and tripod it was attached to jumped to one side, as if someone or something had walked by and pushed it! Adding this to the footage of the lamp turning itself off and on and the door in the main lodge being pushed shut, the night's collected video footage was some of the best the team had ever captured.

Ryan's photos from the theater at the end of the investigation also wielded an intriguing piece of evidence. Once the pictures were downloaded and reviewed, what appears to be the figure of a person standing in the balcony became visible. Although the form is very light, it is distinguishable as a torso and head which cuts off at the top of the balcony rail, revealing depth and showing that whatever this may be, it is standing behind the rail.

Ongoing investigations at the point provide evidence which the UPPRS continues to compile including encounters with fairy lights, disruptions of electrical equipment, and even sightings of doppelgangers, proving Mission Point Resort to be one of the most intriguing locations ever investigated by the team, and possibly the most active location on Michigan's most haunted island.

Superior Impressions

It sits nestled within the shops of the downtown and tourist district of Sault Ste. Marie, Michigan, a sizeable, unassuming, two-story building located at 223 West Portage Ave. At the time of this story, when you walked in, you would be greeted by one of the largest tourist shops in the area. What are now two different businesses, at that time were joined by an opening in the wall, connecting the two. The shop was known as Superior Impressions and was filled with every souvenir, gift, and trinket one could want when visiting The Soo. One side was also a shirt printing shop for every tourist to go home with their souvenir t-shirt, reading, "I Love The Soo," or "I Survived The Soo Locks," or "I Ate Fudge." Whatever a visitor wanted they were sure to find it there.

It was a building that members of the UPPRS had passed hundreds, maybe thousands of times during their childhood years, riding their bikes all around town. They would see the building again during "Slash Ashmun," an activity where local teens drove their vehicles up and down the same downtown roads, windows down, music blaring, and waving at the same group of friends over and over and over again. It was a mundane activity, but a crucial one in the young kids' social calendar. After all, it was where you found out where the parties were, later. Sadly, today this activity is no longer allowed by local law enforcement. But the point is, the team passed this building many times and never gave it a second thought. Until that one day!

One of the shop's managers was someone who knew several members of the UPPRS from back in their high school days, and one day, out of the blue, she reached out to team member Brad Blair.

The message read:

"Brad, how are things? Hey... I am reaching out to see if you, or anyone on the team, have heard stories about the store I manage, Superior Impressions. Wow, have we had some strange things going on, and for a long time. Long before I even started working here, but things have really gotten out of hand lately. To the point where some of my shift managers refuse to be here alone to close up. If you know of any history of the building or have heard of any other possible ghost stories related to the place, can you let me know? Not that I want to scare my employees any further, but just trying to get some idea or understanding of what could be going on. I look forward to hearing back from you! ~ Christy."

Brad's Response:

"Christy, hey, nice to hear from you. Long time no talk. All is well here, and I hope it is for you. It sounds like you have some pretty interesting things happening at the store. Things that the team and I would be very interested in looking into. But I have to be honest; I have never heard a story about that place. I sent an email out to the team, and none of them have heard of any ghost stories related to Superior Impressions, as well. I have to admit, we get pretty excited when we hear of a building in our town that could be haunted, and one we never knew about. Can you share some of the experiences that have happened? And, in the meantime, start keeping a journal of when these events occur. As soon as something happens, write it down with as much detail as you can remember. Make sure to write down the time of day, the date, and the weather. If it was nighttime, then write down the phase of the moon. Everything you can think of, write it down. All of this information helps us when we start our research into something. Thanks for reaching out ~ Brad."

Christy's Response:

"Brad, WOW! I wasn't sure the team would be interested in getting deeply involved with this, but any help you guys can give would be GREATLY appreciated. The place is yours if you ever want to bring everyone in for an investigation. The events that have happened here are a lot, and the last one that just happened will freak you out! The upstairs to this building was an old hotel or boarding house of some kind, but we use it for storage. It's creepy as hell up there! We always hear footsteps like hard-soled boots walking down the hallways. We do know there was one death up there. It was suicide by hanging, committed by one of the tenants when it was a boarding house, and we know in what room it happened. We are always worried that someone broke in and is living up there, but there is never anyone there when we go to check. It's so bad that none of the staff will go up there alone.

"We will be working during the day in the gift shop, and we will hear the shirt embroidery machine turn on and start working WHEN NO ONE IS IN THERE! It got to the point where we had to take the spool of cloth off the machine because we wasted so much product every time it ran on its own.

"Our shop is secured by an alarm system when we leave at night. The night manager sets it, and if it goes off during the evening, an alarm is sent to the City Police. We have had someone from the alarm company in twice now to confirm it is working correctly because of the number of times the police station received the alarm, and every time they arrive at the building, no one is there. Each time, the alarm system has been checked out by the company, and it is working fine.

"There are times when the night manager will be the day manager the next day, and when that happens, they always find stuff moved to a different part of the store. Stuff moving is a constant occurrence. But it's the event that happened last week that convinced me I had to reach out to you. One of the things that our ghost—lol, I feel weird saying that—likes to move is a Christmas caroler figure. In our Christmas room, we have a family of Old English Christmas carolers. A father, mother, older daughter, and younger son. It's the older daughter that is always in a different position or part of the room the next day. Keep in mind that these are good-size dolls. The daughter figure stands about three feet tall.

"Last Wednesday, the night manager was going to be my day manager the following morning. Knowing this, she decided to try something drastic so she wouldn't be freaked out the next morning. While she still had an employee working in the shop, she and the employee took the daughter caroler to the basement and put a box over the top of it. Then they locked the basement door behind them. My manager told me she had a strange feeling leaving the store that night, like she had upset something. It was the fastest she has ever closed up the shop. The next morning she arrived to open the store. As she turned on lights and got the money ready for the register, she was glad to see the caroler was not back in its place. Once the store was ready to be opened, she went to get the doll from the basement. As she opened the basement door, the doll was standing right there at the top of the stairs! She ran out, sick to her stomach, and called me immediately. She would not work the rest of that day. As a matter of fact, I gave her the rest of the week off. Since that story has spread through the employees, it's been tough around here. I guess the more I sit here and lay out all of this, we really could use your guys' help. Please let me know what we need to do to make that happen. Thanks, Brad! ~ Christy."

Brad's Response:

"Holy Shit! You weren't kidding! I am contacting the team right away; we will make this a priority. I will be in touch. ~ Brad."

Sometimes it can take weeks for the team to find a date that works for an investigation. With everyone having careers and families, finding a day and time that works for the majority of the team can be tough. And, the size of the place determines the size of the team. The size of Superior Impressions required the full team to be on hand. When it comes to residential homes where children are involved, The UPPRS will make a quick turnaround for an investigation, no matter what needs to happen. Even though no children were involved with this case, it was apparent a lot of people were being affected and frightened. The group knew this had to be a quick turnaround to get in there, and they made it happen.

A week later, the UPPRS packed up their gear to head into a local building they never thought would be added to their case files. Little did they know this would become one of their more active cases! As the team arrived and received the full tour of the place, they quickly realized the size of the building they would be covering. When the tour was finished, the manager left them with the keys and said, "Seriously, guys, good luck. You are all insane." Not the first time the team had heard this, but they graciously accepted the keys and began unpacking their equipment.

The team chose the room that housed the shirt printing machine as their HQ. If the device were to turn on by itself, well, they would undoubtedly be nearby to witness it! Plus, it was the largest room on the main floor to house all their gizmos, gadgets, and doohickeys. Setup took longer than usual, due to the amount of space the team wanted to cover. With a total of 12 different cameras and many other pieces of equipment set up throughout the shop, the investigation began.

The team's standard protocol is to let their instruments do the work for the first hour. Let the video, audio, motion detectors, and sensors do their thing with no human interference. The team will stay at HQ during this time, going over game plans for the night and letting the energy settle at the location. This night was no different. It was during this time when the famous footsteps were first heard.

"Please tell me someone just heard those footsteps," said team member Jason Fegan.

"Oh, HELL, YES!"

We are not sure whom to credit this quote to, as it was in unison from the entire team. The night was young, and the reported heavy-soled shoes walking through the upstairs hallways had already been heard!

Walking into the upstairs of Superior Impressions is like walking into a completely different building. As soon as you open the door and take the first step up, you leave the brightly painted, well put together gift shop and are greeted with years of chipped-paint history on the walls, darkness, and the damp smell of years gone by. The moment the door closes behind you, you feel like you have been transported in time, and the security of Main Street below is all but gone. Two large staircases lead to the upstairs. One comes from the road and was completely closed off. The other comes from within the gift shop; it was the only way in and out for the night. Once upstairs, you are greeted by a long hallway leading to the right or left. The hallway design is one large square, with two large rooms in the middle and smaller rooms lining the walls all the way around. Once up there, you see and feel the days of it being a boarding house. Small rooms side by side, with what would have been bathrooms the size of a closet. Not the most pleasant of places to live, but for sailors coming off the Great Lakes and looking for a night of drink and fun, this place would have fit their likes just right.

As the team started their ascent, there they were again, the footsteps! This time the steps seemed so deliberate, like someone looking to hide as they heard the group coming up the stairs. The team was sure someone had to be in the building. With a full team on hand, it was easy to split up into groups to check the entire upstairs quickly. Every room, every inch of the upstairs was tested, and NO ONE was there. The night had indeed begun!

Once the area upstairs was secured, and no living person, other than the UPPRS, could be found, team members Tim Ellis, Brad Blair, and Steve LaPlaunt remained while the rest of the team went back to HQ. It was time to get some pictures and EVP work going. As the group went room to room, they continued their EVP questions and taking pictures. They were walking down the hall when they heard a distinct "step and drag" sound behind them. Ellis, who had the still camera, quickly turned and started snapping photos. One practice the UPPRS always adheres to is how they handle still photos. With today's digital and instant images, the team members will snap a picture and wait, not moving an inch. If something appears strange or out of place, they will immediately start shooting multiple photos, knowing they are in the same position as the first photo.

"It's a practice we have used since day one," said Ellis. "I turned and immediately snapped a picture. I waited the split second it takes, not moving from my position, and there it was! This multi-colored mist, or some manifestation coming from the doorway of one of the rooms and into the hallway. I immediately started taking multiple pictures, knowing I was standing in the same spot, holding the camera in the same position, and NOTHING! I could not recreate that first photo."

The trio quickly made their way back down the hall toward the room shown in the first picture. As they turned to look in, that's when it hit them.

"I just remember instant goose bumps," said LaPlaunt. "We were standing directly in the room where the man had hanged himself! The very place that something seemed to be coming out of, or going into, on the picture. And the very area we heard the 'step and drag' noise! These are the moments we wait for as paranormal investigators."

Immediately, Blair fired up the REM meter, a device that allows the team to measure air temperature and electromagnetic fields at the same time.

"You have our attention," Blair said. "You wanted us in this room, and we are here. If you are the individual who passed away here, and you are trying to communicate with us, please drop the temperature in this room."

Within seconds the temperature fell from a warm summer night's reading of 58 degrees to 46 degrees. The room's ambient temperature had dropped 12 degrees, all while the EMF reading was rising.

"You could feel the hair on your neck stand up, and the adrenaline was pumping," said Ellis.

"Okay, thank you," said Blair. "Now, can you bring the temperature back up for us?"

Just as before, within seconds, all the readings went back to normal!

"It seemed as though we had a direct conversation," said Blair. "It was a moment we will never forget. Even though it seemed to go quiet for a while after that, for that brief moment, something was happening. That's often how this field works. There will be a moment of high energy and activity, and then it goes quiet."

After that, the remainder of the investigation seemed to be quiet. There were the usual noises heard, which the team would check out, but nothing that compared to what had happened earlier in the evening. It seemed whatever, or whoever was inside Superior Impressions was done for the night.

Or so the team thought.

During post investigation work, while listening to the audio recorders and EVP sessions, Tim Ellis came across something that made him listen in awe.

"I have always been the EVP guy," said Ellis. "Working in radio and wearing headphones my entire career, I guess it just makes sense. I was listening back from this particular case when I came across one EVP session that to this day is still the best we have ever captured. Team members Matt Barr, Michelle Carrick, and Ryan McLeod were in the basement of Superior Impressions. It's Matt Barr's voice you hear asking the questions."

"Do you live here?" asked Barr.

"Yes," answered the voice.

"Were you a bootlegger?" asked Barr.

"Captain," replied the voice.

"How old are you?" urged Barr.

"Forty-two," answered the voice.

"These replies were not heard at the time of the EVP session," continued Ellis. "It was only in the review that these were found and heard. A full blown, friggin' intelligent conversation! Three straight questions with three consecutive answers! I am still blown away every time I listen to them. The ONLY thing better than capturing something like this would be getting the all mighty money shot of a full body apparition."

So who was this 42-year-old captain who lived at that location? Was he a passerby sailor who rented a room and met his fate after a night of drinking on, at that time, the rough block of Water Street, in Sault Ste. Marie? Or was he something much more?

The post research and application of this case was not done yet, and some historical synchronicity was about to play a role. While doing some research on work the UPPRS was doing for the Whitefish Point Lighthouse, team historian Brad Blair came across some very interesting news.

"I found information on one of the prominent families in the Paradise/Whitefish area of that time," shared Blair. "Commercial fishing was a big moneymaker in the Great Lakes Region, and the Endress family was one of those who were making a fortune. They had their stake holdings in Paradise, Michigan, where the Whitefish Point Lighthouse is located. At some point, the family decided to diversify their holdings and built a building in Sault Ste. Marie that housed a retail dry goods business on the ground floor and a boarding house on the second floor. They sent their son, a captain for their Whitefish fleet, to the Sault to run the new business. The building is the same one that houses Superior Impressions. Sometimes the post-historical research provides the most exciting parts of an investigation. But with Superior Impressions, it was all amazing and fun. It was a case that just kept on giving."

The team shared with the workers at Superior Impressions what they had found, and the history that went along with it.

"Sometimes, just knowing the past and being able to put a living person with the possible spirit that is still with a location can put a person at ease," said lead Tech Lance Brown. "Sometimes, we just have to remind people that ghosts were people once, too."

The team still frequents the location, not to check in on the workers or do follow up research, but because it now houses one of the town's breweries. Soo Brewing Company now occupies half of what was Superior Impressions—the shirt embroidery room, to be exact. The opened wall that connected the two sides has now been closed off, and the other half of the old store is filled with clothing from a retail consignment shop. The tired and worn upstairs that was the boarding house is about to undergo extensive renovations and become market-rate apartments overlooking the historical Soo Locks.

"It's fun to go there and think of what it looked like, and our time there as a team investigating," said team President Tim Ellis. "Although the scenery has changed a lot, we know exactly what we experienced. The events that took place are some of the ones we share the most when we are speaking and presenting at events. The current tenants may or may not be looking for the ghosts, but we know they are there."

So, the next time you visit Sault Ste. Marie, whether it be on one of their perfect July summer nights, their beautiful, crisp fall days, or the winter lovers' paradise, a January afternoon, stop in the Soo Brewing Company and order up a drink. Take a seat in the unique atmosphere of church pews and send a toast to The Captain, eternally 42 years old and still watching over his former holdings.

Cheboygan Opera House

The camera operator stood in the middle of the stage packing away his equipment, exhausted but satisfied with the footage he'd captured of the historical opera house for an upcoming public interest piece to air on the news program that employed him. As he packed the last microphone into its designated place in the tote, he was struck by a spotlight that basked the center stage area in a blue hue.

"I thought we were the only people here?" inquired the news anchor, who had just returned from their van.

"Oh, that's just one of our ghosts," replied the operations director. "They enjoy making themselves known from time to time." A slight smirk appeared on her face.

"Ghosts, huh?"

"Yes. At least two of them, as far as the staff here can tell. Everyone who works here and most of the performers in our live shows have had experiences with them. That blue light turning itself on has become a normal occurrence. We've had it inspected, and nothing wrong could be found. There are plenty of other "incidents" that can't be explained. We've even had a paranormal team from the U.P. come down to conduct an investigation."

"Well, that may be something for an upcoming Halloween episode," the anchor replied, not giving any credence to her tales of specters wandering the corridors.

The following day, as the anchor was piecing together local news stories for the evening broadcast, he was startled by the sudden appearance of one of the station's video production staff.

"You need to come take a look at something," the man said with a bewildered look on his face.

Slightly annoyed at the interruption, the anchor thought about dismissing the young man, but could tell by the anxious look on his face that whatever it was, he felt it was something of importance. As he settled into a seat in the production studio, the video tech pulled up a piece of the opera house footage. As he slowed down footage of the camera panning across the balcony, the anchor discovered what had unnerved him: off to the left, near where the colored spotlights were located, was what appeared to be the transparent figure of a man slowly walking through an aisle of seats. "Huh," he said. "Maybe a Halloween show there isn't such a bad idea after all!"

Months prior to this incident, Brad and Tim gave a presentation at the Cheboygan library as part of a lecture series they present promoting the team, the field, and their podcast, *The Creaking Door*. After most of the guests had left, they were speaking with the event coordinator, and she began a discussion on local haunts including the Cheboygan Opera House.

She told tales of reported phantom guests occupying the theater and unexplained noises coming across the empty stage as well as stage lights turning on and off without explanation. She related that volunteers and caretakers of the historic venue believe a pair of ghosts which they have labeled "husband" and "wife" haunt the theater. The husband has been known to occupy the balcony, and the wife has been seen walking across the stage. They are reportedly friendly and will mischievously play practical jokes on some theatergoers. She definitely piqued the curiosity of the two veteran ghost hunters, and the plans for historical research and a full-blown investigation began immediately.

The name Cheboygan, some say, comes from the Chippewa Indian word Cha-boia-gan, meaning a place of entrance, a portage, or harbor. The mouth of the Cheboygan River was a favorite refuge when the fierce winds of the Great Lakes rose up. The town is bordered not just by the Cheboygan River, but by Lake Huron on the east and the Straits of Mackinac to the north. The dying trade of one industry and the rise of another in the region founded Cheboygan.

In 1844 the fur trade, which had been a staple of the area for many years, started to suffer as regional trading posts shuttered their stores and the long present voyageurs sought new trades. As larger, more powerful ships were constructed, fish became the number one export driving the region's economy. To export fish required barrels, and the demand for lumber to construct them influenced people settling in the region. There was an almost endless supply of white pine, and sawmill operators saw the opportunity for fortunes to be made.

The local lumber industry may have started with the construction of barrels for the fishing trade but it soon expanded to far more. America was building as a nation, and the need for lumber was immeasurable. The forests around Cheboygan were in an ideal location because the downed pines could be floated down the Cheboygan River to be milled, and the finished product shipped to bigger markets, such as Detroit, Chicago, and Cleveland, which all housed ports connected to the Great Lakes.

Saw mills popped up seemingly overnight to meet the demand for lumber. The population of Cheboygan peaked in 1896, which also was the peak of the lumber era.   The Cheboygan Opera House was first built in 1877 through the funding and influence of local lumber barons who not only built large, spacious mansions during the time but also wanted to bring art and culture to the remote area.

The original Opera House was a two-story, wooden structure that quickly became the center for local entertainment, drawing in traveling vaudeville acts as well as offering local performances. Unfortunately, as was often the issue with wooden buildings in the north, which relied heavily on wood burning heating units to provide warmth over the long winters, the structure was destroyed by fire, burning to the ground in 1888.

Undeterred, the city fathers pushed to rebuild the opera house, which would this time be constructed as a three-story brick building. Although more soundly built, the new auditorium was again ravaged by fire in 1903, which burned the top floor of the building. Once again, extensive reconstruction would occur, with the end product being the Cheboygan Opera House that exists today. The building now houses City Hall, the police department, the fire department and the 582-seat Opera House.

In the early 1960s, more and more entertainment options presented themselves. A new generation of families spent their money attending the latest motion pictures at theaters and drive-ins, and many more leisure hours were spent at home watching television. The demand for small town live productions had waned. Requiring extensive upkeep and maintenance, and with less of the public purchasing tickets for its shows, the Opera House was forced to close the doors.

The auditorium sat vacant for many years until the mid-1970s when the Cheboygan Area Arts Council was created and oversaw extensive renovations to the building. Following countless hours of volunteer labor and much financial support from the community, after being closed to the public for 20 years, the restored Opera House reopened its doors on June 24, 1980 and has been a community showpiece ever since.

It was a cold January night when the Yoopers team crossed the Mackinac Bridge, southbound for their investigation of the Opera House. When the team arrived, their first priority, as with many team events, was to eat. They were overjoyed to discover a Bigboy restaurant in Cheboygan, which are getting harder to find. After some pre-investigation fueling on hamburgers, Slim Jim sandwiches and French fries, the team arrived in the parking lot of the Opera House to meet their contact for the evening.

The first impression the team got was of a very modern, three-story building, but upon entering the beautifully restored Victorian Theater, they felt as though they'd walked back in time.

"We enjoy historic venues like the Opera House," Brad noted. "So many people have passed through those halls with such a wide range of emotions. I really think this adds certain energy to the environment, which may contribute to the reported ghostly activity. This place definitely has its own unique aura."

After a tour of the facility, it was evident this would be a daunting task, considering the massive size of the historical building. The team consisted of Brad, Lance, Matt, Matty, Ryan, Steve, and Tim. The group decided to set up home base on a lower level behind the stage in a kitchen area, and like a well-oiled machine began the preparations of setting up equipment for the night.

"This is usually the time of the night Tim disappears," Steve joked. "I believe it's due to his allergic condition to work, and Lance tends to yell at everyone a lot." After approximately an hour and a half of work, logging many stairs and reading base lines, they were ready to go dark and start investigating.

It was not long into the night before the team experienced events. While onstage, two different team members, on two different occasions, heard an unexplained woman's voice coming from back stage. Ryan described his perception of the event: "It was like someone talking in the background. You know they're there but can't make out exactly what they're saying, but it definitely sounded female."

They quickly decided it was time for an EVP session to try to catch the disembodied voices team members were hearing. During the session, Tim asked for a sign that someone was with them and at that moment a rock, seemingly out of nowhere, was thrown across the stage, which they were able to catch on audio. One benefit to investigating an opera house: the acoustics are amazing and even the faintest sound may be picked up!

Tim added, "It was just a small pebble but it sounded like a big rock skipped across the stage. It could have been there all along and one of us kicked it, but considering it came immediately after I asked for a sign of any presence, and the team members were standing still, I would definitely classify this as something freaky."

Also worth noting at this same moment, a temperature drop of seven degrees was registered as compared to baseline readings. Was someone or something stealing energy from the surrounding environment to try to communicate with them?

Continuing their exploration of the Opera House, the team turned their concentration to the balcony. Tim and Matt swept the upper level, taking readings and acclimating themselves to the natural noises of the old theater. The duo decided to take a seat, which they had many to choose from in the abandoned theater, and start the audio recorders. Tim likes to utilize a normal conversation strategy when trying to communicate with the dead.

He says, "In my day-to-day life, I like to talk to people and learn about them, so I let my natural personality lead me during EVP sessions. Some people might feel weird sitting in the dark throwing out questions to no one in particular, but I pretend I am just having another normal conversation. It works for me."

After a series of questions, Tim announced, "We're just here to say hi."

There was a silent pause as he and Matt waited for any kind of response when all of a sudden, over the team's two-way radios, a male's voice came through with a clear "Hello!" It was a strange voice and not familiar to any of the team members. At base camp Brad, Matty, and Lance stopped whatever conversations they were having amongst themselves and looked at each other with inquisitive expressions.

"Who the hell was that?" Lance asked the other two.

The next voice that came across the radios was Matt's. Usually boisterous and loud, he asked in a quiet monotone, "What the f--- was that?"

You could tell from the tone of his voice he was more than a little shaken by the unknown presence making itself known to the team. Unfortunately, despite the group's best efforts, that voice was never heard from again during the investigation.

While remaining in the balcony, Tim and Matt were snapping still photos of the auditorium when they once again heard what seemed to be a voice emanating from the stage area. Matt began a barrage of snapping digital pictures across the entire stage area. A series of these shots shows what appears to be the form of a woman moving across the stage. The UPPRS were aware of the husband and wife that reportedly haunt the Opera House and felt this might have been them reaching out from the unknown.

Matt recalls, "It was a crazy, intense, short amount of time when all these things were happening. You just had this sense that you had tapped into another dimension, one we are not supposed to know about. There was a buzz in the air and the hairs on my arms were standing up. It was definitely one of the highlights of my paranormal career."

During most investigations, the team utilizes motion detectors to identify paranormal activity as well as any human interference from individuals who may be wittingly or unknowingly meddling with an investigation. With the Opera House being attached to the local sheriff and fire offices, as well as city hall, the team thought it appropriate to monitor the adjacent hallway with the motion detector, just in case someone unannounced was in the area and might contaminate evidence.

The motion detector was activated three times during the night, and after investigating each intrusion, the team was positive that no human presence set off the motion alarm. Strangely enough, the third time the alarm went off coincided with Matty asking for a sign of any presence during an EVP session in an area close to the motion detector. Once the device was silenced, Matty followed up with the question, "Do you mind that we are here trying to contact you?" During follow-up review of the audio there was an immediate "No" heard as a clear answer to his question.

Matty reflects, "This was one of our best locations when it comes to EVP work and flat out auditory phenomena. Maybe it is the acoustics of being in a theater all to ourselves, but we were getting hits all night. I remember on one recording there were a few of us sitting around just talking and laughing, and you can hear what sounds like two little girls giggling in the background!"

After a long night of investigating, Tim made the call to wrap things up. Brad and Steve took down cameras and wrapped up cables on their designated orange storage spools in a specific manner to facilitate the next time the team was out. If this task was not completed in a certain way, they would surely hear about it from Lance, the tech manager.

The UPPRS team can be onsite at a purportedly very haunted location, but even when significant paranormal activity occurs during the investigation, when it comes to clean up at the end of the night all minds are on the tasks at hand. Brad and Steve were startled when they encountered one last occurrence to top off the night. As the duo stood next to a restroom door, out of nowhere came a loud bang on the other side, as if someone (or something) had slammed hard against it! The radios, and any other equipment, were in the process of being packed, so it was just the two of them with no way of calling for back up. The adrenaline immediately started flowing as the two investigators quickly switched roles from clean-up crew back to ghost hunters.

Brad slowly opened the door and they entered the restroom to see who or what caused such a large commotion. After checking each stall, they confirmed that no one was in the restroom. They also noted there was no sign of any object hitting the door or lying on the ground near it. They had expected to see damage or at least paint chipped from the interior side of the door, as the unexplained noise they heard seemed so violent. There was no explanation to be found as they backed out of the empty restroom, keeping eyes forward. They continued breaking down equipment, but definitely more on guard of their environment.

Steve exclaimed, "I don't care if Lance is pissed, let's hurry up and get out of here!"

Brad did not reply but his quickened pace showed he was in agreement. This is how the Cheboygan Opera House bid farewell to the UPPRS.

With hours of footage to review and a list full of incidents to be discussed, the guys loaded up their vehicles, feeling the bite of the late night January wind as they did so, and headed back north toward the U.P.

The Yoopers team has been lucky enough to be invited to some amazing sites in their home state of Michigan, and the Cheboygan Opera House, with its rich history and abundant ghost lore, is definitely on their list of favorite locations.

Steve adds, "We are lucky to be surrounded by so much history in this region with such a colorful past that lends itself to potential paranormal activity. Much of it is folklore and local legends, but there tends to be some truth in the legends passed down from generation to generation. I think we feel confident saying the Opera House is a haunted venue. We definitely can't explain some of the things we've experienced here."

The Cheboygan Opera House is open to the public, and you will find a list of upcoming performances at www.theoperahouse.org. It remains one of the UPPRS' most active locations, and they always welcome the opportunity to set up shop for a night to hang out with the in-house spirits.

Ojibway Hotel

The haunted hotel is one of the cornerstones of the paranormal world. Every town, from a rural, one-stoplight community to a bustling urban environment, has a reportedly haunted hotel, motel, resort, cabin or a room for rent. The stories are so prevalent we have dedicated two chapters of this book to such places. It goes without saying that a town as historical as Sault Ste. Marie, Michigan would have a few of these venues. It just so happens that the most historic of the hotels in the history-rich town of the Sault also happens to be the most haunted. The Ojibway Hotel is a local legend and has played host to many dignitaries over the years, including President George W. Bush and world-famous boxer Joe Louis.

The citizens of Sault Ste. Marie can thank Chase Osborn, favorite son of the Upper Peninsula and governor of Michigan from 1911-1912, for the Ojibway Hotel. Governor Osborn believed the Sault needed a hotel of grand stature to attract more visitors to the Upper Peninsula. In 1919, at a hotel convention in New York City, he expressed his feelings on how the Sault was a "golden harvest going to waste until someone with means, vision and imagination shall come and build hotels." He even offered to donate a piece of land to entice potential builders.

After no one answered Osborn's call by 1926, he decided to lead the effort by donating land as a building site. This location is where the hotel still stands today. He also put up $50,000 and challenged people of the Sault to commit additional funds. Osborn's dream came to fruition when the grand opening of the Ojibway Hotel took place on New Year's Eve, 1927.

Governor Osborn did not donate just any piece of land for the hotel project; he donated an extremely valuable piece of property. The Ojibway Hotel overlooks the world-famous Soo Locks and the St. Mary's River, which connects Lake Superior, the most northern of the Great Lakes, with the lower Great Lakes. The St. Mary's River is the only water connection between the upper and lower lakes; however, there is a section of the river known as the St. Mary's Rapids where the water falls 21 feet from the level of Lake Superior to the level of the lower lakes.

Before the existence of the locks, explorers, fur traders, merchants and Native Americans portaged their canoes and any cargo around the rapids. The rapids made it extremely difficult to transport large loads of materials from Lake Superior to southern ports. The natural barrier of the rapids made it necessary for the construction of the Soo Locks. The first lock, completed in 1797, on the Canadian side, was destroyed in the War of 1812. The United States built its first lock in 1855. This provided a safe passage and vital shipping connection within the Great Lakes.

During its first year of operation, 27 vessels navigated the locks. In recent years, nearly 7,000 vessels pass through the locks annually hauling 86 million tons of cargo. The Soo Locks consist of four locks: the Davis, Sabin, MacArthur, and Poe. Currently, all ships utilize the larger Poe and MacArthur locks which can accommodate the largest of the 1000-foot vessels that navigate the St. Mary's River. There is current legislation approved to build another lock, combing the Davis and Sabin into a bigger lock to accommodate all vessels, and have three congruent locks working at all times.

The Soo Locks have been called one of the great wonders of the world and a wonder of engineering. They are a tourist destination for nearly 1 million visitors annually due to the unique experience of watching these huge vessels pass through the locks. However, this marvel of engineering did not come without a price, and there is some dark history attached to its story.

The workforce to build the Soo Locks peaked at around 1700 men. Many were hired from Detroit and other large eastern cities. In addition, newly arrived immigrants were met at the docks and put right to work. This was hard work in hard times, especially during the winter months. An outbreak of cholera hit hard in work camps because of the crowded and unsanitary conditions. By the fall of 1854 as many as 10 percent of the laborers had died while the locks were under construction. Many of the deceased were immigrants, who traveled alone, or left family back home. If they came up missing, there was no one to ask any questions. Out of this, local folktales and legends emerged about people being buried in unmarked graves near the work grounds, including the land where the Ojibway Hotel now stands.

These local legends were one of the reasons the UPPRS had the Ojibway Hotel on their radar to investigate for paranormal activity. However, it was the employee reports of activity that really piqued their interest. A former front desk clerk of the hotel reported that on many occasions they received calls in the middle of the night with requests to change rooms. Guests reported they saw a figure standing at the end of their bed, or the sensation of someone sitting on the bed when no one was there. On more than one occasion, guests checked out in the middle of the night and said they were never coming back. One thing these events had in common was room 616.

When you mention ghosts to Ojibway Hotel employees, many are aware of a spirit named Beatrice, who supposedly was a past owner of the hotel. It has been said that Beatrice was extremely passionate about her job and her hotel. She has been seen in a period style house cleaner outfit roaming the halls, especially the sixth floor. Employees affectionately refer to room 616 as Beatrice's room.

The Ojibway Hotel. Cedit: Steve LaPlaunt.

However, Beatrice may not be alone. Her husband is said to still walk the halls of the hotel with her and has been seen wearing a business

Beatrice. Credit: Steve LaPlaunt.

suit. He will appear out of the corner of your eye, then be gone the next second. Not much is known of him, but the staff refers to him as GIBS, the Gentleman in the Business Suit. Tales of Beatrice and GIBS have been passed down for generations, as many ghost stories frequently are.

A former bartender reports that one night in the Pub area some curious hotel guests were asking about the in-house ghosts. Of course, Beatrice's name came up and after some stories and a few drinks, one of the guests, in a raised voice for all to hear, said he thought it was nothing but people's imagination and that ghosts do not exist. At that moment, a painting on the wall came down and crashed to the floor, the glass frame shattering. The skeptical hotel guest laughed it off, saying it was just coincidence, but he reportedly left the hotel soon after this event.

Dining room staff report there is a utensil drawer in the main restaurant that constantly opens on its own. No matter how many times they shut it and how securely it is closed, it will open on its own. Hotel maintenance staff attempted to rectify this issue, but according to them, there was nothing wrong and no explanation.

One former house cleaner reported a frightening experience while alone on the sixth floor. She had just finished cleaning one room and had moved on to the adjacent room. Most of the floor was empty so the audible flush of a toilet in the room she just left was noticeable; the room that was apparently empty just a few short minutes ago. With trepidation, she reentered the room to again verify it was vacant. She again went about her business when she heard what she thought was the shower curtain drawn across the tub of the same room she confirmed had no living presence. She refused to work alone on that floor for the rest of her shift and avoided being alone on the sixth floor whenever possible.

This collection of ghost stories was gathered over a number of years from UPPRS team members. When they finally got the okay to take a shot at this landmark hotel, they were full of anticipation.

The Ojibway Hotel investigation was broadcast live over the radio as part of the UPPRS's annual Halloween event. The Halloween broadcast is always an exciting time for the Yoopers, but it also comes with the added stress of keeping the listeners entertained. There is no guarantee the realm of the paranormal will cooperate when you are live on the air. Thankfully, UPPRS President Tim Ellis is the host of the radio program, and with his gift of gab and divine voice, he can keep everyone on the edge of their seats for the duration of the show.

The evening would prove to be difficult as the sold-out hotel was full of Halloween enthusiasts, many enjoying adult libations and were in the mood to howl at the moon. The team has learned over the years to adapt to their environment and find a way to procure valid research with the least amount of contamination.

Steve notes, "Many times we've gone into private residences for an investigation expecting it to just be the team and the homeowners.

When we get there, we find ourselves surrounded by the neighbors, the kids' best friends, second cousins and the crazy aunt that sees dead people. So going to work in a hotel full of drunk people, no problem!"

Jason recalls the night at the Ojibway: "It was funny. People were giving us strange looks as we were setting up equipment and running around taking baseline readings. When they found out we were "ghost busters" they all wanted to be our best friends. We had a number of people ask if they could join us, and of course tell us their own haunting experiences. There really is nothing like a good ghost story to bring people together."

The team set up home base in a conference room on the main floor. Because of the distance and amount of foot traffic from hotel customers and employees, running cables for their camera system was not an option. They set up one standalone camera in room 616, Beatrice's favorite haunt, which the hotel was kind enough to grant to the team. Besides that, all other video was done with handheld video cameras. They restricted their investigation to areas off limits to the public, which included the main restaurant, which closed at 9:00 PM.

This was one of the few investigations where the team had a psychic with them, and one of her reported special abilities included table-tipping sessions. Table-tipping is a type of séance in which participants sit around a table, with hands placed on the top. It is very similar to a Ouija board session, but the entire table is the vehicle for communication. Skeptics believe that table-tipping results are due to the ideomotor phenomenon, a psychological phenomenon in which a subject, or group of subjects, makes motions unconsciously.

The psychic, her friend, and three team members (Brad, Ryan and Tim) started the evening with an attempt to contact hotel spirits with a table-tipping session. The rest of the team stood by with anticipation and trepidation as the psychic requested everyone to open their mind and slow their breathing.

Ryan recalls, "I was curious to see what table-tipping was all about and I really didn't expect any results. I was definitely skeptical of the whole event. Once we got into it, I could feel vibrations under my fingertips, which built into a steady hum, and then it felt like the table shifted to my right. It was not an extreme motion, but the table moved. I looked up at Brad and Tim and their faces acknowledged what I was feeling."

Team members looking on in disbelief could not deny what they were seeing—the table did move.

Tim notes, "I have to admit I was really hoping we would have a poltergeist moment with the table levitating off the floor and flying around the room. We did not have anything to that extreme, but I know what I felt, and some kind of energy was causing that table to move. It was definitely a good start to our evening."

As the participants closed the session, they welcomed any spirits that were present to communicate with the team by any means possible during the investigation.

In room 616, the team tried throughout the night to communicate with Beatrice but to no avail. At least that is what they thought. Around 12:30 PM, Lance and Jason went into room 616 to change tapes in the camera. They noticed the camera was positioned on a different angle. Being as tech savvy as they are, they assumed the tripod mount had come loose causing the camera to shift. However, with inspection, they noted it was fitted snug on the mount. They changed tapes and immediately brought the ejected tape to home base to see if they could discern what happened.

Upon review of the tape, the camera appeared to have been bumped, shifting its angle approximately 30 degrees from its original location, which was trained on the hotel room bed, where activity had been reported.

"There were people in and out of that room all night," Lance notes, "but when the camera moved the room was empty. From the way the camera shifted, I think one of the tripod legs had to be moved, as if someone bumped into it. All I can say is, that after reviewing the video and audio, it wasn't one of our team members."

Did Beatrice find a way to reach out to the team?

After the restaurant had closed, and the cleanup was done for the evening, the team made their way into the main dining room, which overlooks the Soo Locks. There was still a lot of contamination due to noise on the streets and the hotel's patrons, but the team made their best efforts to communicate with unseen spirits. The best way to rule out contamination with EVP and Ghost Box sessions is to receive intelligent responses to questions and conversations. Therefore, the team focused on closed-end questions looking for direct responses. During an EVP session, Brad asked numerous questions using his knowledge of the history of the hotel and the Soo Locks, but the simple questions afforded him the best results.

"Were you an employee of the hotel?" Brad asked.

No response.

"Does this hotel mean something to you?"

A disembodied female response of "Yes" was picked up on the team's audio equipment.

"Does the hotel mean that much to you, that you don't want to leave?"

Again a response of a "Yes" was picked up on audio but not audible to any of the team members during that moment.

The ghost box had similar results when team members questioned, "Do you work here?" and "Is this your home?" A clear response of a "Yes" was heard.

Did the team prove the existence of an intelligent entity roaming the halls of the Hotel Ojibway?

As hotel guests made their way back to their rooms to rest their heads, a few obviously ready to pass out from hours of Halloween festivities, the energy of the hotel seemed to wane with the decrease in activity. The last few rounds of team sweeps had no activity to report.

Steve did report the sounds of someone apparently vomiting in the guest restroom on the ground floor, but the team chalked this up to a different kind of spirit that a hotel guest indulged in. With the radio broadcast completed and off the air hours ago, the team started to show their fatigue, so team leader Tim confirmed it was time to tear down.

The Ojibway Hotel, now renamed the Ramada Plaza by Wyndham Sault Ste. Marie Ojibway, is a local icon. The years of history it is associated with are immeasurable. If anyone is looking to take a step back in time, with modern conveniences, of course, this hotel might be just what you are searching for. If you are brave enough, request to stay in Beatrice's room 616. Maybe you will be lucky enough, depending on your point of view, to get turndown service from one of the original owners of the hotel. She may be dead but going above and beyond for customer satisfaction is what she does.

THE VALLEY CAMP

Will Fowler was working the main ticket booth as he noticed an elderly couple, presumably married, approach the window seemingly needing some assistance. He expected the normal questions about the floating museum they were currently aboard or something about the surrounding area; after all, Sault Ste. Marie, Michigan is a tourist town, and questions regarding what to see and where to eat are abundant. After being employed here for 10 years he'd heard them all. The husband, not making small talk, asked, "Is your boat haunted?"

Will was somewhat surprised by the topic but was willing to share what he knew. He replied, "Well, I can't confirm but I've heard at one point in her history there was an accident back in the coal bunker and one of the engineer mates was killed."

The older gentleman asked, "Where is the coal bunker?"

Will replied, "It's back on your way to the engine room."

The wife nodded, as if in agreement.

The husband proclaimed, "Well, she's very sensitive and right in that area she felt something, a presence of some sort, just wanting to make itself known."

Will took in this information without much consideration but was surprised when just a few weeks later another couple came through asking the same question: "Is your boat haunted?"

Will replied with his same response, that he could not say for sure.

The couple listened very intently, and the wife, smiling the whole time, shared with Will that back in the engine room an unseen spirit took her hand and walked her out toward the exit. She described it as being a very benign experience, a sensation of someone offering a helpful hand, if you will. This is life aboard the Ship Museum *Valley Camp*.

Built by the American Ship Building Co. in Lorain, Ohio, the *Valley Camp* was launched on July 14, 1917 as the *Louis W. Hill*. A 1,900 horse power triple expansion steam engine and two coal-fired boilers powered the ship. The *Louis W. Hill* was renamed *Valley Camp* in March 1955 when she was traded to the Wilson Transit Co. During her career the 11,500-ton ship logged three million miles and carried in excess of 16 million tons of cargo.

The *Valley Camp* last operated in 1966, and in 1968 was sold to Le Sault de Sainte Marie Historical Sites, Inc. for $10,000 to become a museum ship. The *Valley Camp* arrived in Sault Ste. Marie on July 3, 1968 and the historical society converted her into a 20,000 square foot museum with over 100 exhibits. Visitors can see how the crew of 29 men lived and worked aboard ship. The museum includes a 1,200-gallon aquarium stocked with various species of Great Lakes fish. It also holds two lifeboats of the *Edmund Fitzgerald* as well as an hour-long presentation about that tragedy that occurred November 10, 1975.

For the past 50-plus years, the *Valley Camp* has resided at 501 E. Water Street in Sault Ste. Marie, Michigan. For the paranormal or

The Valley Camp. Credit: Steve LaPlaunt.

historical enthusiasts, the historical society could not have picked a better location. The Water Street district is rife with the history of integral events and persons that helped shape the town into what it is today. There is also a darker past for consideration if one is willing to look in the shadows. One can explore the location and recreated sections of Fort Brady, built by the United States Army in 1822 to shore up northern fortifications from British incursions from Canada. The fort was built on a 10-acre site facing the St. Mary's River, now Water Street.

Just adjacent to the fort, some might say under it, are the ancient Anishinaabek Indian burial grounds. The shoreline of the St. Mary's has changed considerably over the years and unmarked graves of these indigenous people possibly still remain scattered along the waterfront. In 2005, a fence was established around the perimeter of the burial ground as near as possible to the original boundaries of the site. One can see an example of a traditional spirit house, which was placed over the grave along with burial markers that bore the person's clan symbol upside down, to signify they had passed to the spirit world.

You can also tour the homes of John Johnston, one of the first European settlers to the area, as well as Henry Rowe Schoolcraft, the first Indian Agent in the Sault. As an agent, Schoolcraft became an expert on folklore and mythology of Native Americans, and through his writings about their customs and traditions, provided a greater understanding of the American Indian ways. In addition to learning their ways, Schoolcraft's purpose was also to prepare the local Indian population for a peaceful transition of their lands to the United States.

The Johnston and Schoolcraft families provided one of the Sault's greatest unsolved mysteries. James Schoolcraft, Henry's brother and son-in-law to John Johnston, was gunned down in August of 1846, next to where the *Valley Camp* is now docked, at such close range that he flew right out of his slippers. James was a prominent and influential person in the community, but he also had a darker side, especially when drinking. He stabbed a man in a quarrel in 1830 and was part of several shady business dealings, so he had numerous enemies. The accused murderer was John Tanner, who had threatened some of the area's prominent families, including the Johnstons and Schoolcrafts. No individual was arrested for the crime, as Tanner vanished and was never to be seen again, but some say it was not Tanner at all and he was just a scapegoat. Regardless of Tanner's guilt or innocence, his name was never exonerated.

History has provided numerous opportunities for restless spirits to wander along the Water Street district. When one takes this into account, and you throw in the fact that there is also a large running body of water in the St. Mary's River as well as a hydroelectric plant to one side of the *Valley Camp*, this environment delivers an inexhaustible amount of potential energy for paranormal activity.

Employees of the *Valley Camp* are cautious when asked if their place of employment is haunted, but they definitely seem open to the possibility. Paul Sabourin is the curator of the Valley Camp Museum, and although he reports no personal experiences while roaming the boat on his own in his 10 years of employment, he did participate in a paranormal investigation on board and was privy to some events that may have changed him from a skeptic to a believer. During his investigations, an EVP was captured near the *Edmund Fitzgerald* lifeboat when the name "George" was caught on audio. George Holl was the chief engineer of the *Fitzgerald* when the mighty ship went down. He also reported an individual had a piece of coal thrown at them in the furnace room. "It didn't come from above, it was as if it was thrown straight on from someone standing in front of us." Paul recalled these events with clarity as if they happened yesterday.

Mindy Durham has worked on the ship for nine years and recounts a frightening experience she had one night while closing down for the evening. "I was up top closing all the doors like we do every night," she said. "I looked up and saw someone in the pilot house. At least, I could see the shadow of what looked like someone. When I got there, no one around."

The UPPRS has had the privilege of investigating the *Valley Camp* numerous times and the old ship has never failed to provide them with unexplained experiences that always leave them wanting more. Since the ship is docked in the team's hometown of Sault Ste. Marie, the team has grown up with it as a cultural icon of the region. As their local reputation as ghost hunters grew, people started sharing more and more stories about the *Valley Camp*, which continually piqued their interest. People have reported being touched or their clothes tugged with no apparent culprit. Some have seen shadow figures, while others have been overcome with feelings of an unseen presence on the ship. The team was overjoyed to see what they could find aboard this hometown legend.

Because of her sheer size, 550 feet and multiple levels, the Valley Camp proved to be one of the UPPRS's most challenging investigations as far as total ground to cover. Walking the main deck during an overcast day with rain drizzling down, Jason and Lance were discussing not only the logistics of running cable for the multi-camera DVR system but also how slippery the steel deck was already becoming.

"I'm guessing at least one of us will take a digger before this is done," Lance proclaimed.

"My money is on Matty," Jason replied without hesitation.

The team went into action establishing home base, prepping equipment and setting up cameras in hot spots around the ship.

Due to the size of the ship, the team was able to break into teams and investigate different locations simultaneously without fear of contaminating each other's evidence. Matty, Michelle. and Ryan made their way toward the outside deck to access the galley and crew's quarters. As they entered the crew's dining room, they paused for an EVP session and all seemed quiet.

As they made their way from the dining room to the galley, Michelle gasped. "Did you just see that?" she asked Matty and Ryan. "I just saw a dark shape, like a shadow, walk out the back of the kitchen as we were walking in."

Although they searched, they could not determine what Michelle had seen and whatever it was, the unknown entity was just outside the team's camera ranges. The *Valley Camp* had made itself known to the UPPRS for the first time.

The coal room is located directly beneath the engine room in a cramped, constricting space. Even with the fires of the coal furnaces long extinguished it still has a suffocating feel to it. One can only imagine what it was like when the ship was steaming full ahead and what the crew had to endure stoking the fires. The heat and lack of clean oxygen must have been oppressive to say the least. From previous stories, the team knew this was one of the paranormal hot spots to concentrate on. Brad, Steve and Matt made their way to the stern of the ship and the engine room, then down a set of tight metal stairs to the lower deck. From there they had to squeeze into a narrow passage to gain entry into the coal room.

Matt commented on the oppressive heat as he wiped his brow with a towel.

Not missing the chance to tease his teammate, Steve was quick to point out, "Barr, you sweat in the middle of a blizzard in below zero temps."

Matt replied with his usual comments about Steve being a Cro-Magnon and his hairy knuckles dragging on the ground.

The team, if nothing else, has a lot of fun together, usually at each other's expense.

As Steve was taking EMF readings and Matt was watching a Flir monitor, Brad started an EVP session. All seemed quiet until Brad asked specific questions regarding what it must be like to work in these conditions of extreme heat and toxic air.

Steve thought he heard a response to one of the questions and asked his partners, "Did you hear that? I could have sworn I heard a voice."

Brad or Matt couldn't confirm, but Brad responded, "It's time to wrap up anyway. Let's download the audio to the computer and see if we can hear anything."

The trio handed the DAR off to Tim who was reviewing audio clips on the computer at home base. It is obvious when Tim finds a potential event during review, because his eyes light up like a kid's on Christmas morning, so they knew he must have found something. Tim passed the headphones around so the rest of the team present at home base could hear. During the EVP session, when Brad asked, "Was it hard to breathe with the heat and coal dust?" we could hear an immediate response in a voice that was not Brad's, Steve's or Matt's. The response to Brad's question was, "I am coughing." It was not clearly audible to the group but the next voice heard was Steve proclaiming he thought he heard something. The potential of an intelligent haunting roaming the depths of the boat immediately became apparent to the group.

Another paranormal hot spot of the ship is an area of reverence in honor of the *Edmund Fitzgerald*. The legend of the *Edmund Fitzgerald* is one of the most famous of all shipwreck tales regarding the Great

Lakes. The accounts of that fateful night of November 10, 1975 are widely known through books and media of all sources. Canadian folksinger Gordon Lightfoot kept the ship and its doomed crew in our memories with his 1976 song, *The Wreck of the Edmund Fitzgerald.*

The *Edmund Fitzgerald* was lost with her entire crew of 29 men on Lake Superior 17 miles north-northwest of Whitefish Point, Michigan. Few major artifacts have been recovered from the night she sank to the bottom of Lake Superior, but two of them are located on the Valley Camp Museum. Two lifeboats from the *Fitzgerald* are on display for all to see and remember. One is ripped in half, showing the pure force and fury of the greatest of the Great Lakes. One cannot help but stand in the presence of the two lifeboats and feel the raw emotion of sadness and respect for those who lost their lives and the families and friends forever affected by that fateful night. Numerous visitors have reported a heavy feeling in this area. Many are surely overcome by emotion, but other, more sensitive people feel something we cannot ascertain with our normal senses.

During the team's investigations they have used all the equipment they have at their disposal, but one item they have had luck with is the ghost box. Brad, Jason, and Ryan had been in the lifeboat room for the better part of an hour monitoring temperature and EMF readings, along with conducting EVP sessions and were seemingly having no response to the atmosphere and environment they so thoroughly were monitoring. They decided to try their luck with the ghost box, and the trio threw questions out into the dark hoping for a response. As the ghost box was spitting out unintelligible nonsense and white noise, Brad informed the group it was time to head back to home base. He finished the session with a heartfelt "thank you." "We're going to head out for now but thank you for allowing us this time aboard your ship. We truly appreciate it."

Just then, an audible "You're welcome" came across the ghost box that all three team members could make out without question. As the three made their way toward the upper decks, they could not help but smile knowing someone had apparently been listening to them.

As a long night aboard ship came to an end, Lance and Steve were in the theater room fighting the late night/early morning urges to close their eyes.

"You ready to start packing up? This is going to take a while," Steve asked Lance.

Lance replied, "Yeah, I think everyone is ready to call it a night. This is Steve and Lance saying goodnight. We want to thank you for allowing us to be here with you tonight. It was an honor and we look forward to coming back."

As Lance reached for the ghost box to stop scanning the airwaves, they heard "Goodbye" come across loud and clear. Lance looked at Steve and did not have to ask if he heard that; he could tell by the look on his face.

"I think that's a good place to leave it," Steve responded to Lance's unspoken question.

Another event the team members experienced while onboard may not have a paranormal theme, but it was a profound experience, nonetheless. Tim, Ryan, and Matty were in the *Edmund Fitzgerald* lifeboat room conducting an EVP session and using an actual recording of the last transmission the *Fitzgerald* made to the *Arthur M. Anderson* on the famous night she sank.

On November 9, 1975, Captain Ernest M. McSorley and the *Fitzgerald* sailed away from Superior, Wisconsin loaded with 26,116 tons of processed iron ore, heated and rolled into marble-size balls. The ship *Arthur M. Anderson*, captained by Bernie Cooper, joined her and they pulled away from dock around 2:30 PM. The *Fitzgerald* was a faster ship and was ahead of the *Anderson* by 10 to 15 miles. Aware of a November storm reportedly heading their way across the Great Lakes, Captain McSorley and Captain Cooper remained in radio contact throughout the voyage.

As weather conditions continued to deteriorate, gale warnings issued on November 9 had been upgraded to storm warnings early in the morning of November 10 with winds gusting to 50 knots and seas 12 to 15 feet high. These were treacherous conditions to say the least, but both captains were experienced and had safely navigated this body of water in similar conditions many times before. At 3:30 PM, November 10, Captain McSorley radioed Captain Cooper and said, "*Anderson*, this is the *Fitzgerald*. I have a fence rail down, two vents lost or damaged, and a list. I'm checking down. Will you stay by me till I get to Whitefish?"

McSorley was decreasing his speed to allow the *Anderson* to close the distance so the ships were closer in case they needed each other. Captain Cooper reported at 6:55 PM that the *Anderson* was rocked by a huge wave. "Then the *Anderson* just raised up and shook herself off of all that water—barrooff—just like a big dog. Another wave just like the first one, or bigger, hit us again. I watched those two waves head down the lake toward the *Fitzgerald,* and I think those were the two that sent him under."

Morgan Clark was first mate of the *Anderson* and was maintaining radio communication and watching the *Fitzgerald* on radar. First Mate Clark spoke to the *Fitzgerald* one last time, about 7:10 PM:

"*Fitzgerald*, this is the *Anderson*. Have you checked down?"

"Yes, we have."

"*Fitzgerald*, we are about 10 miles behind you, and gaining about 1 1/2 miles per hour. *Fitzgerald*, there is a target 19 miles ahead of us. So the target would be 9 miles on ahead of you."

"Am I going to clear?" answered Captain McSorley.

"Yes, he is going to pass to the west of you."

"Well, fine."

"By the way, *Fitzgerald*, how are you making out with your problems?" asked Clark.

"We are holding our own."

"Okay, fine, I'll be talking to you later." Clark signed off.

The *Fitzgerald* disappeared from the radar at 7:15 PM.

First Mate Clark called the *Fitzgerald* at 7:22 PM. There was no answer.

The above conversation played repeatedly inside the *Fitzgerald* lifeboat room onboard of the Valley Camp Museum. As Tim, Ryan and Matty listened to the voices of the doomed crew, they could not help but feel a mixture of sadness, fear, and anguish.

"We are holding our own."

As the words of the transmission still resonated in a room where the remains of the *Fitzgerald*'s lifeboat sat, they heard from Lance, who was monitoring the team's home base of operations. He radioed down to tell them to get to the top deck immediately. Lance, knowing what his teammates had planned for the EVP session, tried not to let the emotion he felt show in his voice. Tim, who would usually be annoyed by being interrupted during such an important investigative technique, sensed the urgency in Lance's voice. Tim and Matty emerged from the lower decks not knowing what to expect or why Lance interrupted their EVP session. As they walked outside, the full ramifications of the moment hit them.

Tim recalls, "Looking off the stern of the ship we saw the *Anderson* heading down the St. Mary's. The *Arther M. Anderson,* still in active service, was right there in the middle of the St. Mary's River. After the emotions of the EVP session, I was just speechless. It was not paranormal, but it was crazy to see this ship passing us at the exact moment we were playing that recording. It was one hell of a coincidence that not only gave me chills but brought tears to my eyes then and still gives me chills just thinking about it today."

The *Valley Camp* has provided the Yoopers with some great experiences, and they consider the ship an ongoing investigation in their case files. If someone were preparing a ghostly road map of locations necessary to see, the Valley Camp Museum would have a big star next to it. You can immerse yourself in history and get a real onboard experience of life aboard these amazing vessels. One never knows if while touring the ship some unseen force will grab your hand and help you along your way.

STONE HOUSE, DRUMMOND ISLAND

The old caretaker cautiously advanced up the stairway. He knew he was alone in the old mansion, the seldom-present owners having returned to their fulltime abode far south of rural Drummond Island and Michigan's Upper Peninsula. The last of the seasonal tourists were gone and no new tenants would occupy the house until spring arrived. He knew he was alone, so why was he hearing footsteps on the hardwood floors above?

Although somewhat alarmed by the creaking boards, this was not the first time he'd encountered what sounded to be someone walking through the vacant rooms of Stone House Mansion. When he conducted his search, it was always with the same result; he was greeted by quiet emptiness. No burglars or unwelcome wildlife were invading the place, just the peaceful stillness of an old house. Sure, there was that antique rocking chair that seemed to have a mind of its own, occasionally turning up in the rear of the back bedroom, kitty-corner from its regular placement next to the bed, but there had to be a rational explanation for that, just as there had to be for the footsteps, he always reasoned.

He had never been superstitious and paid no attention to tales of the island's supposed ghosts and goblins that were told around campfires on dark summer nights. Besides, there were no deaths or tragedies associated with the house that he was aware of. But something felt different this time; a heaviness to the air. As he made his rounds, checking one room after another, he was relieved to find everything in order. "Must be the wind pushing through those trees," he said aloud to himself, explaining away the sounds that necessitated his search of the upstairs. Making his way toward the stairway, relieved to be heading home for the night, he came to a sudden halt.

Directly to his right, on the staircase leading to the third floor, something caught his eye. Frozen in place, he watched as what appeared to be the shadow of a man slowly ascended the stairs and disappeared into the top floor. Before he could even attempt to rationalize what he had just observed, he found himself racing down the stairs and out the door. He tore down the gravel drive in his truck, the Stone House disappearing in his rearview mirror.

Stone House Mansion, or just the Stone House, as the structure has long been referred to, due to its predominately rock-walled exterior, has stood as one of the premiere structures on Drummond Island for more than a century. It was constructed during the second wave of settlers to the island, following a brief occupation by the British military.

Drummond, which sits at the northern point of Lake Huron, was named for Lieutenant General Gordon Drummond, who was the commander of all British forces in Canada during the War of 1812. Believing the island to lie in Canadian waters, the British erected a fort in 1815, becoming the first Europeans to settle there. Thirteen years later, the fort was abandoned as the British were forced to leave the island, which was now officially in American territory. This would be the final piece of American soil ever occupied by the British.

Drummond was virtually unexplored in those days, heavily wooded and populated only by wild animals and a few Native Americans during the summer fishing season. Its remote location made it an ideal place for anyone trying to avoid detection by the outside world, especially the area where the Stone House now stands. Prior to the arrival of the British, this stretch of waterfront, known as Scammon Cove, became the preferred hideout for one of the most feared pirates to ever sail the Great Lakes, Captain Juan Eduardo De Rivera, and may possibly be home to his long-hidden treasure.

De Rivera began his career at sea in the mid-1700s as cabin boy to a notorious band of Cuban buccaneers. They taught him the art of navigation as well as strategic raiding and pillaging. By the 1780s, he was leading his own crew of marauders in the Gulf of Mexico, competing with other bands of pirates who were also engaged in the plundering of Spanish and American ships.

As competition grew fierce, and often deadly between waring pirate crews, De Rivera sought to leave the Gulf. He had heard tales of prosperous settlements far north on a group of lakes which were referred to as The Inland Seas. Although the ships supplying these ports were not likely to be hauling the gold caches that were the desired booty of Spanish ships in the Gulf, these lakeside communities were mainly unguarded and, for a group of well-trained marauders, ripe for the picking! Hence, in 1793 Captain De Rivera would sail his schooner, the dreaded *Dimante Negro* (the Black Diamond), north to an area where both competition and military protection were sparse.

De Rivera's crew made quick work of plundering these small communities with a simple formula: raid by night, under cover of darkness, and hideout during the day. When the attacks were against settlements of northern lakes Michigan and Huron, that daytime hideout was Scammon Cove. With its deep water bay, a small island blocking the view from the main trade route on Lake Huron, and bountiful wild game and fish to feed the crew, Scammon Cove enabled the *Dimante Negro* to anchor for prolonged periods without worry of detection. The unexplored forest provided the ideal location to stash the plundered goods until they could be sold off for profit.

So went the days of De Rivera and his crew: terrorizing the settlements of the Great Lakes region. Their largest hit came against the people of Cleveland in 1799, a ruthless raid conducted on a Saturday morning, which secured his place as the most wanted criminal on the lakes.

He would hold this title for another decade until 1809, when, sailing up the Detroit River, the *Dimante Negro* found itself surrounded by four military gunboats. Acting on reported sightings, authorities had set the trap for De Rivera, making sure there was no chance of escape. The crew, realizing there was no way out of the blockade, rowed out on a skiff, surrendering to authorities. De Rivera, in true outlaw fashion, refused to be taken alive. Legend has it he strapped his legs to a detached anchor on the ship and, in a last defiant gesture, loosed the anchor from the *Dimante,* releasing it to the bottom of the river, and sending him to a watery grave.

But was this truly his demise? Surely, a trained mariner such as De Rivera would have no problem cutting loose the ropes and swimming away, undetected as the commotion of the surrendering pirates drew the attention of the authorities. Could it then be possible that he would make his way north to a secluded location known by few others, to live out his days in a wilderness which had provided an undiscovered sanctuary to him and his crew so often in the past?

De Rivera may well have made Drummond Island his final home. Legends still abound of buried treasure near Scammon Cove, and the ghost of the pirate captain who stalks the beach at night, protecting his still-hidden plunder.

It wasn't the lure of hidden pirate treasure that would bring the next explorers to Scammon Cove, but the riches to be gained through harvesting the forest itself. In 1870, Chicago financier group Hitchcock and Foster received news from one of their scouts of a large, untouched track of cedar forest they had discovered on an unsettled island in northern Michigan. The company was quick to lay claims and sent William Hitchcock to the island to establish what would become known as the Island Cedar Company. A new flock of settlers followed Hitchcock to Drummond to earn their living in the lumber trade, and they were not just lumberjacks. An operation of this scale would require mill workers, cooks, bookkeepers, shipping agents, store keepers, and all the support staff required to run a large commercial operation. An entire village sprang up practically overnight.

By the early 1880s, the area around Scammon Cove began to look more like a boom town than the remote wilderness the company scouts had discovered. The village boasted tracks of housing, a general store, post office, and many of the modern conveniences of the day. The mill operated in 10-hour shifts six days a week, with products easily shipped out via the natural deep water port the cove offered, to be sold to developing communities throughout the Great Lakes region.

In 1892, after 20 years of nearly non-stop harvesting, the cedar of the island had become depleted. The company was forced to make a tough decision, one that would impact the lives of every man, woman, and child who had come to call Scammon Cove home. Hitchcock would close down the mill, moving the Island Cedar Company to the nearby mainland village of De Tour, where it would be re-established as the De Tour Cedar and Lumber Company.

Many of Hitchcock's employees followed him to the mainland, the lure of guaranteed employment at the new location outweighing the attachment to their homes and the lives they had built on Drummond. The few who remained, however, would not have to wait long before the buzz of the sawmill and life as usual returned to the cove.

Shortly after Hitchcock relocated his cedar business, the island mill and properties were sold. Harold Johnson, another entrepreneurial lumberman, saw that although cedar had become sparse, the island still offered a vast wilderness of hardwood trees that could be harvested for lumber, shingles, and other goods. The H.C. Johnson Company was formed, which not only employed the remaining citizens of the cove but recruited new workers to fill many vacant positions and newly created jobs, as Johnson began buying up land across Drummond. At one point, it was estimated that he owned a full 25 percent of the island, the majority of it still covered by virgin forest.

The village around Scammon Cove experienced another boom, with rail tracks being laid and new docks constructed to ship out larger quantities of finished product. At the height of the lumber trade, it was estimated that the island housed the largest year-round population it would ever see, even to this day.

During this period of expansion, the aging Johnson sold a portion of his company to a new business associate, the man responsible for construction of the Stone House, Mr. Charles Wood of Tonawanda, New York.

Wood was the owner of Wood and Brooks, a prominent manufacturer of piano keys and actions with factories operating in Buffalo, New York and Rockford, Illinois. While scouting new lumber suppliers, Wood discovered the Johnson Company, located in an area which could easily ship to his plants via schooner over the Great Lakes. He and his new business partner would come to name the settlement around Scammon Cove, which was now wholly owned by the company, Johnswood. When Wood eventually bought out Johnson, the company name was also changed. The former H.C. Johnson Company became the Kreetan Land and Lumber Company, with Wood naming himself as president, dictating that he spend more time overseeing the daily running of the operation.

Wood had mixed feelings about island life: he harbored great affection for the northern wilderness and the outdoor activities it afforded during the summer months, however he had no desire to be stranded at what inevitably became a remote outpost when the winter months set in and the lakes froze over. After great discussion with his family back in New York, a compromise was reached: he would relocate the family to Scammon Cove during the summer, operating both of his companies from a location which served as a midpoint between the Illinois and New York plants, and return with them to their primary residence in New York when autumn arrived.

Prior to the Wood family abandoning city life for summers on the island, a home worthy of their lifestyle needed to be constructed; a structure suitable for not only family life, but also for entertaining affluent guests. Charles selected a piece of land on Scammon Cove, overlooking the waters that once harbored pirate ships and British scouts. In 1913, crews began construction of what would come to be Stone House Mansion. The main house, surrounded by 45 acres of unspoiled wilderness, boasted eight bedrooms, four bathrooms, three large fireplaces (two on the main floor and one in the master bedroom), and the "Eagle's Nest," a large third-floor room offering breathtaking views of both the cove and surrounding forest. The well-manicured grounds sported a grass tennis court, boat house, and 1,300 feet of sandy waterfront. In the wilds of Northern Michigan where small cottages with outhouses were the standard domestic structures of the day, this was not just a house, but a status symbol as well.

For more than a decade, the Wood family spent summers lounging and entertaining at their seasonal home, leaving the hustle and bustle of the city during the hot months and enjoying their woodland retreat and all it had to offer. In 1918, fire heavily damaged the company mill, but it was quickly rebuilt and upgraded, providing for more capacity during the still booming years of the lumber trade, and adding to the family's wealth.

As time progressed and new technologies and infrastructure spread throughout the country, the lumber business on Drummond began to wane. Increased competition and better roads with modern vehicles made it easier for new mills to spring up, which were no longer dependent on shipping finished goods by water or rail. By the late 1920s, the Scammon Cove mill was operating at minimum capacity and the village of Johnswood was quickly becoming a ghost town.

Families and businesses either left the island or relocated to newly developing areas, away from the vast tracks of lands owned by the company. Many homes and businesses were disassembled; the hardware and lumber salvaged for new structures on other parts of the island. Little trace would remain of the once thriving lumber town.

The Wood family maintained ownership of the company properties on Drummond until shortly after World War II when Charles' son Elton sold the majority of these lands to the State of Michigan. The final piece of property held by the family was the 45-acre plot on which the Stone House sits.

As the village that was once Johnswood became reclaimed by nature, trees growing up where stores and homes once stood and vegetation overtaking the abandoned town cemetery, the Stone House sat empty. Peeling paint and an overgrown lawn were the sight which greeted visitors to the property, making it the perfect setting for a ghost story, which it quickly became. Passing boaters reported seeing lights turning on in the empty house and more than once a spectral figure was said to be seen walking along the waterfront, disappearing into the now-dilapidated boat house; stories which quickly spread among the island community.

After sitting vacant over a number of years, new owners arrived to breathe life back into the grand manor, as they refurbished the mansion into a bed and breakfast, marketing its natural beauty and seclusion to tourists looking for a retreat from everyday life, much as it had been for the Wood family long ago. It would eventually become a vacation rental, which it is operated as today, leasing out to guests on a weekly basis from spring through fall.

When the current property managers, Galen and Sheree Terry, asked the UPPRS to investigate the strange happening at the Stone House, it was more out of curiosity than fright. The former caretaker had not hesitated to relay his stories of phantom footsteps and the shadow figure on the stairway that had frightened him out of the house years before, and they had experienced a number of their own odd occurrences.

Not long ago, Galen had been called by the family renting the place to deal with an issue they were having. They stated that when they left that morning the door to the back bedroom had been wide open. Upon returning, they found it not only closed, but locked from the inside. Puzzled, as the only lock on the door was a sliding bolt, Galen retrieved a ladder and climbed up to the second-floor window, which had luckily been left open. As he stepped off the ladder into the room, everything was found to be in order. There was no sign of any intrusion, yet just as the tenant had claimed the door was locked; the slide bolt mechanism, which could only be operated from inside the room, pushed securely into place.

Then there were the incidents told to them by the crew of a Canadian fisheries organization which rented the mansion as a headquarters one month while doing research in Lake Huron. They had returned one evening, hungry and exhausted after a long day of working on the lake. Lounging in the dining room, the men were startled to hear the kitchen door open. Glancing into the room to see who could be entering the house, they all viewed the door standing open for a moment, as if being held by an invisible hand, then slowly closing on its own. Intrigued by the incident, but too tired to pay it much mind, the group finished dinner and decided to call it an early night, leaving their youngest member, Jason, to clean the kitchen. Dawn came early this time of year, and their research necessitated the group be on the water and collecting data prior to the first rays of sunlight hitting the lake.

After finishing the dishes and turning off the lights, Jason made his way to the top of the stairway. Just as he reached the second-floor landing, the door to the master bedroom slammed open against the hallway wall! Derek, the team supervisor, emerged from the room, clearly disturbed and clutching his belongings. "No way in hell am I spending another night in that room!" he muttered. Jason noticed the other crew members were now peering out their doors, nobody uttering a word as Derek stormed down the hall, claimed one of the smaller vacant bedrooms, and quickly slammed the door, locking it behind him.

The next morning, Jason and the others were already in the kitchen making breakfast when Derek emerged from the second floor. "Well, I guess you guys are wondering what happened last night," he said. "I've been trying to figure out how to explain it without sounding crazy. It's that damn picture!" The crew sat silently, all knowing the painting he referred to. Above the bed in the master bedroom hung an antique portrait of a woman. When the group had first checked in, one of the guys joked about it looking like something out of a horror movie, which may not have been far from the truth.

"While I was getting ready for bed, something about that room didn't feel right," Derek continued. "Didn't matter where I was, the eyes in that painting seemed to be watching me. I thought it was just my mind playing tricks on me, but when I crawled into bed and glanced up, the eyes weren't staring out at the room like they should have been, but straight down at me!" he concluded. As incredible as it sounded, no man on the crew spoke out against Derek, who was known for his no-nonsense demeanor. For the remainder of their time there, no one set

119

foot in the master bedroom. The portrait has since been removed from the Stone House.

Some of the purported hauntings were not relayed first-hand to Galen or Sheree but found written out in the mansion's logbook. These musings range from sounds in the basement to brief sightings of Katrina, as the female spirit has come to be called, working in the yard or walking the beach. The following excerpt from the log was written by a group of 18 friends from southern Michigan who had rented the house for a summer vacation. They wrote:

> We enjoyed reading all the other entries and stories of Katrina. Had some good laughs about those stories and then shit started getting real.
>
> Loretta was reading a book she brought from home. She put in her bookmark and put the book aside to go eat dinner. When she went back to continue reading, her bookmark was in the back of the book and a laminated bookmark of bible verses was inserted at the correct page.
>
> Sherri slept in the Eagle's Nest and felt a presence next to her at night.
>
> By then we all agreed to leave the stair light on because it is so freaking dark at night. But it was off whenever anyone needed to use the bathroom. We figured it was one of us playing a joke until we were all sitting in the living room and the stairway light went on by itself.
>
> One of the people in our group is an Indian Shaman. He smudged the house and nothing else happened after that.
>
> If you see or hear from Katrina, tell her we all said hi!
>
> P.S. Our last night we were sleeping in the Eagle's Nest. Heard a creak on the steps and it sounded like someone was crawling on the floor. I reached for my phone for the flashlight and when I turned it on, whatever it was, it was gone!

Sheree, being a paranormal enthusiast, was intrigued by these stories and decided to conduct a ghost hunt of her own. She invited a friend and their husband to join her as she tried to catch Katrina or any other spirits on audio recorders and cameras. While working her way through the rooms of the first floor, Sheree saw her friend's husband exiting the house through the side door. Thinking nothing of it, she continued on to the second floor where she came face to face with…the husband! "I just saw you walk out the door! How can you be up here?!" she exclaimed. With no explanation given, the doppelganger would be the only (albeit impressive) strange occurrence to cross their paths that night. Sheree was now convinced; these occurrences were far outside the realm of normalcy, and no deductive reasoning could explain them away.

She contacted the UPPRS that summer, hoping to get them to the island for a thorough investigation of the property. Being an active vacation rental, and one that tends to be booked solid through the summer months, she would have to wait until October before giving the Yoopers full run of the Stone House for the investigation; an investigation which would prove to be well worth the wait.

It was a chilly afternoon when the team headed south, through the canopies of red and gold leaves that attract so many tourists to the area that time of year, grateful to experience the natural beauty autumn displays in their part of the country.

With a calculated dinner stop worked into the plans, the team kept a close watch of the time during the ride down. Drummond Island is only accessible by a car ferry which runs hourly. If they were even one minute late, they could be stranded in De Tour Village, waiting on the ferry for the next hour, and losing precious investigation time.

All went according to plan and as the team rolled off the boat they were greeted by Galen and Sheree who guided them around the island to the night's venue. When the pavement ended and the road turned to a narrow gravel trail framed by overgrown forest on either side, they hoped their destination was near, and they weren't taking an impromptu off-roading trek through the woods.

Following a brief drive down the wooded trail, the team pulled into a sizable clearing. They were greeted by a large, well-groomed yard bordered by sandy Lake Huron beach frontage. In the center stood the mansion, constructed mainly of native stone and rising almost as high as the white birch trees that grew between the house and waterfront. Down a short path at the far side of the yard lay the grass tennis court, now nothing more than two metal posts in an obviously man-made clearing, slowly being overtaken by the bordering forest.

Crowding through the side entrance, the team received a tour of the house from Sheree, including the history of the area, legends of pirate treasure and long-passed staff members of the mill said to haunt the property. She detailed the unexplained occurrences they needed to be aware of and where in the house events were most often reported. With the briefing complete, Sheree and Galen took their leave, letting the team get down to business.

As the guys began scouting camera placements and unloading equipment, Brad located the log book and undertook the tedious task of reviewing years of entries from past tenants. As he skimmed through page upon page of vacation memories and promises to return for another North Country getaway, he flipped to a page that was anything but pleasantries. There, scribbled on the page before him, read the following:

Somehow, we survived unspeakable horrors that lie beneath. During the darkness, always keep a candle with light, lest the basement come to you.

Next to the anonymous lines was a sketch of something that appeared to be a dark entity. After re-reading the words several times, and studying the crude drawing, Brad shook his head and "Kids," he thought. "Has to be a prank." The figure in the drawing bore too much of a resemblance to the demons of Hollywood horror flicks to be taken seriously. But still, could this journal entry have been influenced by an actual occurrence? In any case, it was worth sharing with the rest of the team.

Brad rejoined the group at their makeshift headquarters in the dining room and related the tale of the Basement Demon and several other newly discovered incidents; mainly brief statements jotted down of possible paranormal happenings intertwined with pleasant vacation stories. The team had just finished setup and were preparing to break into groups for the investigation. There was plenty of territory to cover; not only were there three levels and a basement, but with activity reported outdoors, the grounds needed to be worked as well. In vintage Scooby Doo fashion, the guys split up to search the old mansion.

Tim and Jason, drawing the short straw, would be the first to work the yard. It was late in the season and the sunset came early, and the cold breeze coming off the water was anything but pleasant. "We'll start with the tennis court and then work along the waterfront," said Tim, grabbing an audio recorder along with a hat and gloves. Jason followed with a camera and EMF meter.

Reaching the tennis court, Tim initiated an EVP session, in hopes of partaking in a conversation with an unseen participant. After a stretch of unanswered questions, he began to wrap things up when a crashing noise echoed from the nearby forest. They continued with the questioning, in hopes the sounds had been produced by a lingering spirit in answer to their requests.

"Looks like the only thing you managed to summon was a trash panda," Jason said, pointing to the small furry raccoon scurrying out of the trees and across the far end of the court.

"Yep, and even he isn't interested in hanging out with us!" replied Tim.

"Let's start working our way back to the house. Maybe we'll get lucky and see a ghost ship on the way," Tim joked, as the two headed towards the beach.

As Tim and Jason inspected the waterfront, the last rays of the sun vanished. With flashlights pointing down to illuminate the beachside trail, Jason spotted something sticking out from a grouping of rocks. When he bent down to inspect the object, a feeling of apprehension shot through him, causing him to hesitate before touching the item; it was a rough piece of wood, approximately eight inches long, with

123

what appeared to be a female figure sketched into it. Retrieving it from the stones, he decided it was worth bringing into the house for closer evaluation. As he continued, he saw Tim just ahead on the trail, bending down to grab something.

"Check this out," said Tim, reaching his arm out toward him.

Jason gave a wide-eyed gaze to the object in Tim's hand. Tim was holding a nearly identical chunk of wood, this one sketched with a male figure. Were these effigies of some sort, or simply an art project abandoned by a former tenant? With both wooden curiosities in their possession, they made their way back indoors.

Inside the house, the remainder of the team had spread out to explore the reported hot spots. On the second floor, Matty and Ryan were moving room to room, careful not to trigger the motion detector that sat behind the door in the back bedroom. If it closed on its own tonight, the shriek from the alarm would alert everyone in the house. This same room housed the purportedly haunted rocking chair, known to relocate itself when the house was empty. Painters tape was placed around the bottom of the chair in order to discern any movement during the night.

Meanwhile, Brad and Steve finished a check of the ground floor and headed for the cellar. "Guess we better get to the basement before it comes to us," Brad joked, referring to the ominous log entry.

"You think there's something to that?" asked Steve, as they descended the creaky wooden stairs.

"Nah. Probably just kids screwing around. But...guess we'll find out soon," answered Brad as they entered the dark, empty space.

Settling into the front area, Brad pulled out his audio recorder and was about to begin an EVP session when Steve interrupted. "Shine your light on the back of my neck," he demanded. "What's on me?"

"Nothing" answered Brad, flashlight now honed on Steve's back. "It felt like a spider just ran down the back of my head. I could feel it moving, and when I reached back, it ran down my neck!" Steve, not known for exaggerations, had obviously felt something.

"Well it's gone now," replied Brad. "Want me to radio upstairs for some bug spray?" he asked sarcastically.

Returning his attention to the audio device in his hand, Brad pushed the record button and was again ready to start the EVP session when the recorder let out a shrill screech and went dead. "Batteries are shot." said Brad. "We put new batteries in everything while you were screwing around with that logbook."

"Can't be dead," replied Steve.

Before they could speculate on why the device had shut down, their two-way radio came alive. "Did one of you guys just walk by the camera?" It was Lance, who had been watching the monitor from headquarters.

"No, we're in the opposite room from it," answered Steve.

"Something just went past it. Looked like a large dark mass," Lance returned.

"Maybe the basement is coming to us." Brad joked, albeit nervously.

The two made their way to the opposite end of the basement, checking on the camera and searching the vicinity around it. The room was dark and empty but felt much colder than the adjacent area they had just left. After a few minutes spent in silent observation, the sound of an object hitting the wall and bouncing to the floor put them back on alert. Their flashlights scoured the cellar floor in search of the source of this latest disruption, but nothing could be found.

As the rotation came to an end, the two started for the stairs, reviewing the occurrences of this shift: Steve's sensation of being touched, batteries suddenly draining, and the dark figure crossing the camera all happened within the course of less than a minute. Was that by coincidence? It seemed the basement may have indeed come to them.

When the team regrouped in the dining-room-turned-command-post, activity reports were exchanged and everyone had an up close look at the figures Tim and Jason had recovered from the beach. "Let's set an EMF detector next to them and see if they give off any signs of energy," suggested Lance. "Being solid pieces of wood, the meter shouldn't pick up anything."

After a quick debriefing and snack break, the team went back to work. Jason remained in the dining room, settling in for camera duty; the table holding the monitor now sharing the space with bags of chips, trail mix, energy drinks, and half empty bottles of water.

As Jason sat through his shift, catching the occasional view of the guys entering and exiting the rooms as they appeared on the split screen feed of the monitor, something caught his eye. Off in the corner where the wooden effigy blocks were set, the EMF detector began to light up, indicating an energy presence in the immediate area. He gazed over for a bit, and as nothing else occurred, turned his attention back to the monitor. Then it happened again; the meter lit up and continued to do so in uneven intervals. His first thought was that one of the field groups was either above or below that area, using equipment that could be setting the meter off. He grabbed a two-way radio to check their locations.

After the two groups inside the house radioed in, confirming that they were nowhere near that end of the building, Lance's voice came through the speaker: "We're down by the waterfront working an EVP session. No way are you picking anything up from us."

With piqued curiosity, Jason shot back, "What are you asking down there?"

"If anyone associated with those wooden blocks would communicate with us," was the reply. "Not getting any response, though."

"You might be wrong on that," replied Jason, gazing over at the blocks.

At Jason's request, Lance immediately returned to the house. He had a theory. Jason felt the outdoor EVP session may have elicited responses from the wood blocks that stood in the corner. The two compared the timing of the questions from the beach to the times the meter had registered energy readings. As predicted, almost every spike on the meter matched one of Lance's interactions with his audio recorder; a reminder that communications come in many forms.

Meanwhile in the upper levels, Ryan and Matty had worked their way to the Eagle's Nest. They had spent most of the current rotation on the second floor; hosting nonresponsive EVP sessions, checking to see if the haunted rocking chair had moved (it hadn't), and snapping pictures which showed nothing out of the ordinary.

Matty lay down on one of the many beds lining the wall of this single, large room which comprises the entirety of the third floor, and Ryan settled into an easy chair across from the staircase. "Wake me when it's time to pack up," Matty joked.

"Let's get one more EVP session in, then head back down," suggested Ryan.

Matty sat up, armed with a digital recorder and a K2 EMF detector. Ryan utilized his Ovilus, a device which randomly displays words, presumed to be manipulated by ghostly forces, hoping to experience some type of activity before the investigation came to an end.

Matty began the final inquisition of the night, anticipating another one-way conversation. "Something about sitting in the dark and talking to yourself can really make you question your life choices," Ryan mumbled sarcastically when it was his turn to chime in. Noticing a small opening in the ceiling Ryan asked, "Is there anything above us?" The question was greeted by both a spike in Matty's K2 Meter and a response displayed on the Ovilus' screen: ATTIC. Both men shivered as the room suddenly became very cold. "What's in the attic?" Ryan continued. A deeper chill ran through them as the screen presented a single word: NOOSE.

The conversation continued, the lights of the meter seemingly answering their questions, as the room continued to grow bitterly cold. Matty, attempting to shake off the unnatural chill, began to walk across the room when he noticed Ryan's eyes shoot toward the stairway. Looking to that direction, Matty stopped dead in his tracks. "Holy s#@t! There's a shadow by that doorway!" As the shadow figure shot across the room, Matty stumbled backwards, landing squarely in Ryan's lap. "Did you see that?!" Matty shouted, the figure having disappeared down the stairway.

"Yah, now get the hell off of me!" Ryan replied.

Gathering up their equipment, the duo hurried down to the second floor, radioing in to the rest of the team, who joined in on a thorough search of the upper levels. With no further appearance of the shadow figure and nothing out of the ordinary occurring, the investigation had come to a standstill.

Brad, who had been dozing off on a living room couch prior to the radio call, seemingly ready to call it a night, pointed out the time. "If we want to catch the next ferry back to the mainland, we need to start tearing down now. They only run every-other hour overnight, so we better not miss it." It had been an eventful outing, but it was time to wrap things up.

As the crew sped off to catch the boat, equipment hastily packed and loaded, the last thing any of them wanted to think of were the hours of recordings which needed reviewing. When all was analyzed, there were some intriguing bits of audio; the sound of an object falling in the basement, a vague voice captured in the master bedroom, but nothing to confirm if they were in the presence of Katrina, Captain De Rivera, Charles Wood, or some other spirit of Scammon Cove. And unfortunately, the shadow man had evaded their cameras. This would all be discovered in the coming week. For now, the team hurried toward the ferry dock, and their dark journey home.

Houses of Spirits: Haunted Bars

No matter what you call it, pub, tavern, lounge…a bar is a bar. People gather there to celebrate, to mourn, to catch up on the day's news and gossip, and sometimes just to relax and have a drink. With the wide range of emotional energies poured out in these places, it's no wonder so many of them house more than one kind of spirit. Wander into any bar which has existed for more than a few decades and ask the bartender to tell you about their ghosts. Chances are you'll be in for a treat! It may be an unexplained banging noise from an empty cellar or a misty figure stooped at a corner booth, but any good barkeep will invite you to pull up a stool while they relay some supernatural experience which happened to them, a colleague, or predecessor.

The UPPRS has investigated (and patronized) their share of bars over the years. These outings offer different challenges than the average case, with timing being one of the major factors. Most bars in the U.P. serve customers until two in the morning and have staff closing up during the following hour. In many cases, this means an investigation won't begin prior to 3 AM, putting the team under a major time crunch considering that the majority of these establishments are located in business districts with heavy morning traffic beginning around 7 AM or earlier.

Another complication, although now outlawed in Michigan, is the "smoke factor." When patrons are smoking cigarettes throughout the night, the remaining smoky haze in the air plays havoc on any visual evidence, often leaving false positives of "misty forms."

It can be all the worse when the owners are not completely forthcoming with the conditions of the location. One such case occurred when the team traveled south at the request of a tavern owner to investigate their purported haunting, being assured that the place would be closed by midnight and prior to that, the upstairs apartment, which was nearly soundproof from the barroom below, could be investigated.

Upon arriving, the Yoopers were shown the main entrance to the upper floor, a narrow staircase covered in nearly a foot of snow! After spending time shoveling, equipment was hauled up and positioned for the first segment of the night. As more and more patrons arrived and the jukebox started playing, it became painfully obvious that the second level was far from soundproof, and audio equipment would be useless until the bar emptied out.

As midnight approached, the team readied their equipment to relocate to the barroom and kitchen areas of the main floor. Having worked through various investigative techniques with no results, it was nearly time to descend to the public area where most of the reported activity occurred. Twelve o'clock hit, and the music continued to play, the parking lot still filled with trucks and snowmobiles. When one o'clock rolled around, Tim and Brad checked in with the bartender who assured them all customers were leaving shortly and they would then have full run of the place. Just after 2 AM, the parking lot cleared out and the disgruntled ghost hunters made their way downstairs, finally able to begin the investigation.

The kitchen staff had complained of nervous feelings, as if someone were watching them as they worked, and several of them reported hearing a growling sound while they worked. Upon entering the room, Steve's EMF meter spiked and remained at maximum levels throughout the entire room. "No wonder they feel uneasy," he said. "They're working in a fear cage back here!" This is an environment where the electromagnetic frequencies are consistently at a high level, due mostly to outdated wiring or antiquated electronic equipment, which can cause feelings of paranoia and in extreme cases lead to skin rashes and hallucinations. The growling sound was also quickly debunked, as the team experienced it themselves and noted that it occurred in conjunction with an old compressor in the basement, grinding itself into action, likely seeing its last days of usefulness.

As vehicles drove past, the team noticed that their headlights reflecting off a billboard across the road sent quick flashes of light through the main barroom. The "white figure" frequently viewed at night out of the corner of the bartender's eye had been explained.

After spending another hour in dead silence, the guys packed up and headed for home, confident that the "paranormal activity" reports had been debunked. At the very least, explanations could be given for the occurrences which the owners had reported.

Fortunately for the Yoopers team, most investigations aren't accompanied by so many hang-ups, and many U.P. bars offer great historic intrigue, as was the case when they were contacted by another concerned proprietor. The call came from Mary Lou Harmon who, along with her husband Rich, have owned the Raber Bay Bar & Restaurant since 1986, and have experienced their share of unexplainable occurrences on a frequent basis throughout the years.

Raber Bay is a small fishing village on the shore of the St. Mary's River, just north from the passage connecting the river to Lake Huron. At the turn of the twentieth century, it was home to a large sawmill which employed a great number of people, boosting the area's population during its years of operation. As so often occurred with early mills, a fire broke out in 1913 and consumed the entire operation. Although many of the villagers were forced to relocate in order to find new employment, some remained, taking various jobs in the remaining lumber and fishing industries.

In 1931, the building which now houses the Raber Bay Bar and Restaurant was constructed as a dual purpose facility: village post office and dining establishment. As was often the case during Prohibition years, these small town restaurants often served a dual purpose of their own, operating as eatery and speakeasy. Such was the case in Raber. Being situated on the Canadian border, it was a simple matter to purchase alcohol from the bootleggers who smuggled the booze across in boats with little contention from revenuers, who seldom patrolled these rural territories.

These first years of operation were some of the liveliest in the bar's history. Hollywood icon Mae West, who vacationed on neighboring Lime Island and was rumored to have friends in the "organization" that transported illegal alcohol across the border, was known to drop in for drinks, and graced the patrons with a few songs in her signature contralto style. Lumberjacks and fishermen bellied up after a hard day's work, and were happy to have a place to unwind, raise a glass, and enjoy top-rate entertainment in the rural north woods.

Although the post office is long gone, the bar and restaurant are still in business. A landmark in the eastern Upper Peninsula, Raber Bay caters to not just the local population, but the summer tourist trade and winter snowmobile traffic alike who return year after year for the fresh fish and frog legs, and to enjoy spirits of many varieties.

When Mary Lou contacted the UPPRS, it was with no shortage of haunting tales to tell. In the years she and Rich have owned the bar, everyone from staff, patrons, and even freight drivers had witnessed what they believed to be paranormal occurrences.

"One day, our milk order was being dropped off," Mary Lou recalls. "The driver was bringing the cases in the delivery entrance when a garbage can rose off the floor, hovered for a few seconds, and dropped back down. He couldn't get out of the building fast enough!"

Some staff members report the feeling of being watched, and occasionally must deal with their names being called out from an empty room. Banging noises from the kitchen and the apparition of a man they consider a "mischief maker" are also regular experiences which come with the job.

It was a Monday night in the fall when the team packed up for the trip to Raber Bay. Being the slow time of year, the restaurant was closed on Monday, void of both staff and patrons, providing ideal conditions for investigating. The sun set around 7:30, allowing for the team of Tim, Brad, and Ryan to begin their work early without the distractions reflected sunlight can cause; always a concern when the location has large windows, even more so when they face the waterfront, as is the case in Raber.

As the guys pulled into the parking lot, they were met by Mary Lou along with a long-time employee and friend. As setup commenced, the two women filled the team in on even more ghostly sightings that had taken place, adding to their eagerness to get underway with the night's work. With cameras set, batteries checked, and equipment laid out on a high table in the corner of the barroom, it was go time!

Following a check of EMF levels and noting natural "noise makers" (ice machine, compressors, etc.), the trio sat at separate tables in the dining area, placing a K-2 EMF detector at each. Following a brief, uneventful EVP session, Ryan pulled out his phone and checked the signal strength. Working in remote areas of the U.P., this is never something to be taken for granted! Fortunately, the cellular towers were in the team's favor that night, and Ryan was able to connect to web service.

Taking into account the location's history, Ryan downloaded a stream of vintage music by none other than Mae West. As West's unmistakable voice joined the notes of a trumpet and piano, a second session was begun. "If you recognize this voice, let us know by touching one of these boxes on the tables," Tim said. Not only did one of the K-2 meters light up, but lights on all three sequentially flashed to life and dropped back down, as if triggered by an invisible hand moving in order across the room from Ryan's table, to Brad's, and over to Tim's.

"Were you present during the 1930s?" "Do you have a direct connection to this building?" "Do you make yourself known to the staff?" The questioning continued, with at least one of the meters reacting to each of these inquiries. When the K-2s remained dark for a period, the audio recorder was stopped and reviewed: once again, no voices answered the lengthy session, but the energy readings observed were enough to intrigue the investigators and the two women, who were observing the team from the next room.

The night advanced and the team attempted various experiments, including attempts to recreate the banging noises reported from the kitchen, with no luck. They were moving into a storage area in a far rear corner of the dining area when the EMF meter spiked and held steady for a few seconds. As the indicator dropped back to zero, the guys were startled by a series of five distinct knocks on the wall behind them, seemingly emanating from the building's exterior. Ryan rushed out the closest door, confirming that nobody was near the building, thus eliminating the possibility the raps were caused by pranksters trying to mess with the investigators.

When the night neared its end, the guys agreed to conduct one more EVP session before wrapping things up. "Let's get the ladies involved on this one." Brad suggested. "Whoever is here would probably rather speak to them than us." After a few rounds of questions from the now-expanded group, Brad wandered back to the equipment table and took out the ghost box, a device not used on every investigation due to its controversial nature. It's basically a broken radio which continually scans frequencies, but the team had acquired some interesting results in the past, and any data collected can be helpful to a case.

After familiarizing the new participants with the box, the group took turns asking questions. When Tim was up, he asked, "Is there a reason someone banged on the back wall earlier?"

The crackling noise seemed to rise in pitch as the words SOMETHING HIDDEN were discerned by the team. After failing to get any clarification on this, Mary Lou asked, "Who are you?"

Again, the box chimed in, this time the name PETER was clearly heard by everyone present.

Mary Lou let out a gasp, visibly startled by the response. "Peter was the name of the original owner, the man who built this place. Peter Kott," she revealed.

"Are you the man who built this bar?" Brad inquired, prompting the final answer received that night: THAT'S CORRECT.

It's easy to understand why a person who put so much of their life into creating a business and dedicated their blood, sweat, and tears to make it successful may want to stick around for a while and keep an eye on things, but when the spirit haunting your favorite watering hole is a complete unknown, the mystery involves deeper digging.

The Satisfied Frog has operated in Sault Ste. Marie, Michigan under many names throughout the years, the current title being a twist on the previous name of The Horney Toad Lounge. Built in 1896 as a fur company trading post, the building has served as a boarding house, retail store, and telephone company, but has spent the vast majority of its life as a tavern.

When Christy and Bruce Bardaville bought "The Frog" in 1995, they undertook an extensive remodeling project, renewing the interior walls of exposed stone and reclaimed barn wood and constructing an addition to the rear of the historic building. It was after the rehab had concluded that the new owners realized they may have unseen tenants. "Whenever I was in the building for more than a few minutes I would start to feel drained of energy," Christy recalls. "This lethargic feeling would stick with me until I left, and then things were fine again."

Christy was not the only one to claim an odd experience in the bar. Staff members began reporting a variety of strange happenings: nickels appearing on recently cleaned tables, the laughter of a young girl emanating from an empty restroom, and a reddish figure appearing near a sealed up tunnel in the basement, once part of an underground network used to move liquor during Prohibition, were all occurring on a regular basis.

The Satisfied Frog. Credit: Steve LaPlaunt.

"I've been getting stock from the basement and felt somebody brush across my back," claimed waitress Katti Messerschmidt.

136

The Horney Toad bar at the Satisfied Frog. Credit: Steve LaPlaunt.

"Sometimes, when counting tips at the end of the night, I can feel someone breathing on the back of my neck. Just like in the basement, when I turn around nobody's there."

Employees also feel a strong female presence, most notable at closing time when the bar emptied out, who they affectionately named Sheila. Although most activity didn't unnerve the bartenders, the red figure in the basement was an exception. Although not exactly malevolent, the atmosphere accompanying its appearance caused great unease.

With activity ramping up, Christy reached out to two psychics in hopes of discovering why these disturbances were occurring. Given no details of the happenings, the women spent a lengthy amount of time exploring the building. When they finished, they joined Christy to deliver their findings. On the second floor, which was previously a boarding house but now sits vacant, they claimed to sense multiple energies, none of which wished to interact with the living. The main bar area is home to two spirits, a male they refer to as Mel, and a female, which Christy informed them was well known to her staff as Sheila.

The sensitives felt that Mel was a Prohibition-era gentleman who had ties to the bar. He was there to keep an eye on the place and would occasionally mess with electronics. Sheila was a young native Canadian woman who moved to America as a maid and nanny for a prominent family. Any connection to the bar is unknown, but she enjoys the atmosphere and takes pride in seeing women succeed in society through opportunities she was never allowed. Neither Mel nor Sheila causes any intentional problems at the Frog, and both enjoy the Up North atmosphere of its location.

Overall, the spirits they sensed within the building were nothing of concern, with one exception: the basement dweller. When the psychics descended into the cellar, they were immediately drawn to the area of the sealed tunnel, the domain of the red apparition. Describing the specter as "bordering on malevolent," they were in agreement that it was a male spirit who had lived a less than charitable lifestyle and was afraid to cross over, fearing retribution for the actions of his lifetime. Although they claimed they were not able to convince the entity to move on, they were able to get him to leave the building and felt that he followed them for a brief period afterward. No further sightings of this ghost have been reported since their visit.

The UPPRS became involved with The Satisfied Frog when a customer contacted the team to review a photo she'd taken on her phone the prior night. Kasey, the young lady with the photo, explained that she had snapped a pic of her two friends in the bar. When they viewed the image, they saw accompanying the two young women was a disturbing anomaly, a gnarled, disembodied hand! The hand, which vanished just past the wrist, seemed to be grasping the shoulder of the lady standing to the left. The sight unnerved the women enough that they left the bar and avoided returning for months. Hoping to find explanations for this episode and the plethora of occurrences related to team members by the staff, the guys arranged for an investigation.

It was a blustery winter night when the group set out in search of answers to the Frog's reported hauntings. Arriving just past midnight Tim, Brad, Ryan, and Matty piled their gear in the basement and bellied up to the end of the bar where they would wait for the remaining customers to exit. Ironically, the movie *Ghostbusters* had just begun on the television nearest them, providing entertainment for the guys and extra ammunition for the remaining patrons to crack jokes at the teams' expense.

When it became obvious the last of the clientele were hanging around in hopes of watching the investigators at work, Christy signaled last call and sent them on their way. Setup began, and as Brad ran cable up to the door leading to the second floor, the first obstacle presented itself: the door was locked and no key could be found.

"I could kick it in," Matty offered jokingly.

After an extensive but fruitless search, the team gave up hopes of working all three floors and set up cameras and equipment on the two accessible levels.

The investigation began with Ryan and Brad hitting the basement first. After thumbing through stacks of old beer posters and bar mirrors, the two conducted a ghost box session, listening to the unintelligible noise as long as they could stand it, with no discernable words being presented. After a flat EVP session which also returned no results, they began to make their way to the stairs when a burst of light caught Ryan's eye. "What just happened?" he asked, puzzling over the sudden illumination.

"I'm not sure. There aren't any light fixtures in that corner." Brad answered as he made his way toward the walk-in cooler where the pulse had appeared. As he entered the dark corner area, a box slid off the top of a pile and landed at his feet, just as the indicator on his EMF meter shot up. Another EVP session was hastily begun in hopes that communication could now be made, yet again no voice appeared during playback.

Upstairs, all was quiet. Tim and Matty, along with Christy, had just finished an EVP session while using an Ovilus. None of the words which appeared on the device's screen were relevant to the case, and no unseen visitors left audio on the digital recorder. Brad and Ryan related what had happened in the basement, frightening Christy a bit, as she feared the red figure had returned. Ryan was quick to reassure her that the light surge had no tint to it and wasn't of any recognizable form.

Tim Ellis, left, and Matt McLeod conducting EVP sessions at the Satisfied Frog.

The teams switched up areas and continued to investigate. Unfortunately, this was one of those nights where things remained quiet and before the first rays of sunshine hit the snowy sidewalk out front, the group had packed up their cases and called it quits. They did, however, leave the camera system hooked up and running through the remainder of the nighttime hours. Brad would return to collect it prior to business hours the next afternoon.

When the additional video footage was reviewed, all appeared normal, with the exception of one brief flash of light, eerily similar to the vibrant pulse Ryan and Brad had experienced in the basement earlier in the night. The case remains open, and the Yoopers continue to visit the bar. Occasionally, they even investigate!

Considering the sheer number of historic bars in Michigan's Upper Peninsula, it's hard to believe that more haunted taverns won't present themselves to the UPPRS for investigation. Although unique circumstances and tall tales often accompany these early morning cases, the team is always happy to pull up a stool and see what spirits may present themselves.

AFTERWORD

The field of paranormal research has changed drastically since the founding of the Upper Peninsula Paranormal Research Society. With the advent of the "reality television" genre, the realm of the supernatural has expanded from something only covered by the media during the Halloween season to a year-round entertainment source, with many cable networks featuring programs revolving around the paranormal. New theories and methodologies present themselves with each new wave of para-reality programming, making the field seem a little less taboo to the average person viewing these events safely from the comfort of their living room sofa.

The UPPRS has evolved over the years as well. In 2008 the team became a Michigan Non-Profit Corporation, allowing them to conduct their work on an official level and also to team up with philanthropic groups to aid in fundraising efforts for various charitable organizations and offset the costs involved in their field investigations, which remains a free service to this day. The following year they established the Michigan Paranormal Convention, an event which has become one of the nation's most respected gatherings of paranormal enthusiasts and experts, taking place annually every August in the team's hometown of Sault Ste. Marie, Michigan. In 2014 two of the group's founders, Tim Ellis and Brad Blair, jumped into the broadcasting ring with the creation of their podcast *The Creaking Door Paranormal Radio,* which can be downloaded for free through many platforms including GooglePlay and Slackjawpunks.com, and features the latest in paranormal news stories as well as interviews with some of the biggest names in the field of paranormal research.

As much as things have changed through the years, the mission of the UPPRS remains the same: to research possible incidents of paranormal activity, provide rational explanations where they can be found, and offer support to those affected by these seemingly unexplainable occurrences. The team remains the tight-knit group of friends who began their journey into all things strange so many years ago and they continue that trip today.

The stories contained in this book were chosen by the team as some of their favorite investigations into reported hauntings of public locations. Although there have been many private residences that have wielded uncanny stories and activity over the years, they have been left out of this volume in order to ensure the privacy of the individuals involved.

The Yoopers team hopes you've enjoyed this look into their slightly creepy, sometimes comical, and often misunderstood world and reminds you that, whether you lean toward the side of skeptic or believer, an intrigue of the unknown may open the door to your next great adventure!

ACKNOWLEDGEMENTS

Through the years of research and investigations, the UPPRS has been blessed with an amazing support system of people who have helped out on many levels. Without these groups and individuals, many of the cases covered in this book would never have been possible. They would like to take this opportunity to thank all of those who have aided in their pursuit of the strange over the past several decades and give special kudos to those who have gone above and beyond in contributing to this book.

First and foremost, the team members who comprise the Upper Peninsula Paranormal Research Society: Tim Ellis, Steve LaPlaunt, Brad Blair, Lance Brown, Jason Fegan, Matt Barr, Ryan McLeod, Michelle Carrick, and Matt McLeod. The UPPRS team exemplifies the old saying of "The family that plays together stays together," and that's what the group has become: a family. Together through good times and bad, with plenty of play time mixed into the work.

The family members of each of these individuals also must be thanked. Living in the same home with people who sacrifice their weekends, stumble into the house at daybreak, and lock themselves away for hours at a time to review footage from the last investigation is not always easy. Each of you deserves a great amount of gratitude for your support and understanding through the years.

Don Hermanson of Keweenaw Video Productions, affectionately referred to as "Uncle Jesse," has become a defacto member of the Yoopers team. His production of two commercial video projects featuring the group, 2008's *Ghost Hunting With the UPPRS* and 2012's *Ghost Hunting at Mackinac,* both of which document investigations appearing in this book, lead to his joining the team on more field investigations. His support throughout the years has been unwavering.

145

Not only has Ben Duff volunteered his time and insight toward the team website and social media sites, he has also offered an extra set of hands on numerous field investigations and provides an extra "tech" opinion on collected evidence.

The director of the Gulliver Historical Society and "keeper" of Seul Choix Point Lighthouse, Mrs. Marilyn Fischer and her support staff, including Bob and Jean Williams, have always welcomed the team with open arms to what has become dubbed their Paranormal Disneyland. A truly beautiful location that is paranormally active, yet always welcoming.

Galen and Sheree Terry, property managers of the Stone House Mansion on Drummond Island were a great help in both welcoming the team to investigate and contributing source material for the Stone House chapter in this book.

The directors and staff of the Great Lakes Shipwreck Historical Society who operate the Whitefish Point Light Station along with the Great Lakes Shipwreck Museum do an amazing job at preserving the maritime history and culture of the Great Lakes region. They have graciously welcomed the UPPRS in for multiple investigations of their campus.

Sault Historic Sites' Paul Sabourin and the staff of the Museum Ship Valley Camp were graciously forthcoming with both the history of the ship and their personal experiences onboard. The Valley Camp is one of the teams' favorite hometown haunts.

The Kinney family who owned the historic Antlers Restaurant for many years were very gracious not just in having the team in for multiple investigations, but also to allow them to film their work for public projects.

The Michigan Paranormal Convention would not be possible without the unwavering support received through the years by the staff and management at Kewadin Casino and Convention Center and the UPPRS's partnership with the Sault Convention and Visitor's Bureau and their staff, with special thanks going out to Linda Hoath, Debbie Goeschel, and Mariah Goos, who go above and beyond year-round for the event. Special thanks also to all of those who support MiParacon through their attendance every August. It couldn't happen without you!

Jeff Belanger has been gracious enough to offer up his thoughts and suggestions on this project, and more than a few jokes along with them. His input was greatly appreciated.

The Godfather of ghost hunters, John Zaffis, has offered his guidance and knowledge to the UPPRS for many years. His direction and support, in the early years and today alike, continue to be valued and greatly appreciated.

This book would likely never have come to fruition without the encouragement and guidance of Rosemary Ellen Guiley, both throughout the writing process and beyond. It was her proverbial "kick" that started the project in the first place, and she deserves much credit for putting up with three rookie writers coming together for their first collaboration.

Lastly, many thanks go out to all of those who have opened up their homes, businesses, and lives to the UPPRS over the years. The team remains always humbled by the trust placed in them by clients who are looking for answers to the things they cannot explain. It is an honor that is always taken with the utmost respect and sincerity.

Bibliography

Arbic, Bernie. *City of the Rapids: Sault Ste. Marie's Heritage.* Allegan Forest, MI: The Priscilla Press, 2003.

Bardaville, Christy. Interview with Brad Blair. Personal interview. Sault Ste. Marie, MI, February 1, 2019.

Brumwell, Jill. "The Island We Know as Drummond." *Great Lakes Pilot,* September 2018.

_____."The Island We Know as Drummond: Scammon Cove 1870's." *Great Lakes Pilot,* October 2018.

Fischer, Marilyn. *Spirits at Seul Choix Pointe.* Gulliver, MI: Seul Choix Press, 2013.

Gringhuis, Dirk. *Lore of the Great Turtle.* Mackinac Island, MI: Mackinac Island State Park Commission, 1970.

_____.*Were-Wolves and Will-O-The Wisps.* Mackinac Island, MI: Mackinac Island State Park Commission, 1974.

Harmon, Mary Lou. Interview with Brad Blair. Personal interview. Sault Ste. Marie, MI, November 5, 2018.

Hermanson, Don. *Ghost Hunting on Mackinac Island.* Houghton, MI: Keweenaw Video Productions, 2012.

_____. *Ghost Hunting With the UPPRS.* Houghton, MI: Keweenaw Video Productions, 2008.

Kelly, James and Dean Sandell. "Historic Scammon Cove." Drummond Island Tourism Association. https://visitdrummondisland.com (accessed December 8, 2018).

Kluck, Kevin and Randy Kluck. *Yooper Bars.* Sault Ste. Marie, MI: Whiskey River Publishing Company, 2011.

Longtine, Sonny. *Courage Burning.* Marquette, MI: Sunnyside Publications, 2006.

Lowe, Kathryne. "As I Remember Johnswood." *The Weekly Wave,* August 16, 1972.

McAdams Huttenstine, Jan. *Remotely Yours.* Paradise, MI: East West Press, 2010.

Nute, Grace Lee. *The Voyageur.* New York, NY: D. Appleton & Co., 1931.

Schoolcraft, Henry. *The Hiawatha Legends.* Philadelphia, PA: J.B. Lippencott & Co., 1856.

Stevens, Deidre. *Thunderstruck.* Sault Ste. Marie, MI: Deidre A. Stevens, 2005.

Stonehouse, Fred. "Do Ghosts Walk at Whitefish Point?" *Lake Superior Magazine,* November 2007.

Terry, Galen and Sheree Terry. Interview with Brad Blair. Personal Interview. Sault Ste. Marie, MI, October 26, 2018.